Sacred Spirit of The Gorge
Columbia River Gorge Flower Essences & Essences of Place

copyright © 2017 Camilla W. Bishop
Sacred Spirit of The Gorge: Columbia River Gorge
Flower Essences & Essences of Place

copyright © 2008, 2010 Camilla W. Bishop
revised edition of Listening to the Wildflowers:
Guide to Columbia River Gorge Flower Essences

ISBN-13 978-1542619110

Nature Spirit Publishing
NatureSpiritAlchemy.com
CamillaBlossom.com

Sacred Spirit of The Gorge

Columbia River Gorge Flower Essences
& Essences of Place

Camilla Blossom Bishop

Nature Spirit Publishing

The Hopi prophesized that on August 16, 1987, 144,000 Sun Dance mystical teachers would help awaken the rest of humankind to a spiritual awareness. The same date marked the end of a 28,600 year cycle in the Cherokee calendar; the age that follows is called the Age of Flowers, a time when the essence of flowers will be recognized and used more as healing and spiritual agents.
—internet source

If we could see the miracle of a single flower clearly, our whole life would change.
—Buddha

The flowers are keys to the survival of the species as they open the way for the coming changes—the unfolding of paradise.
—Danu, the Fairy Queen

Life must blossom like a flower offering itself to the Divine.
—The Mother

Loving & Receiving: A Solstice Epiphany

It is almost fantasy to think that the world is exploding with colorful blossoms of iridescent and rainbow flowers yet that is what I feel deep inside. My heart breaks open again and again to a new state of elegance—a deeply sublime inner frequency as if to remind me of true paradise in the making.

I was so sure my meanderings were going towards familiar places yet when I reach the next state of being I am without gauge or compass in this new terrain of spirit. It feels so deliciously cool and electric and comfortable all at the same time.

My fondness for flowers elevates all my wanderings to colorful blossoming Truths. Nothing can be truer than a flower. Its surrendering is its opening. Its radiance is beauty itself. It does not need anyone present to make it more. It is all it is meant to be.

A flower radiates its frequencies compassionately towards the One. If we choose we can receive its gifts without any need to reciprocate, but we want to. We want to understand how much we can radiate our beauty and serve in that way. And receiving nourishment is easy. We live to soak in rain, sun, wind, earth, and fill up with that which makes us grow.

—Camilla Blossom Bishop, June 2007

Table of Contents

Nature Awakenings 1
Wildflowers are Calling... 7
Creating the Columbia River Gorge Flower Essences...................... 9
The Columbia River Gorge 10
Sacred Water 12
Medicine of the Flowers 13
Healing with Flower Essences 17
As Complementary Therapy..17
Safety..18
Flower Essence Therapy 18
How to Take Flower Essences 23
How to Select Flower Essences.. 27
Dowsing: Finger Testing & Using a Pendulum 29
Creating a Flower Essence Formula 30
Preserving Flower Essences 31
How to Make Flower Essences 33
Channeling & No-Pick Method 36
Elements in the Wildflowers... 39
Earth, Fire, Water, Air, Ethers in Flowers............................... 39
Flower Families 41
Plant Healing Signatures...41
Lily Family 41
Asteraceae or Composite Family 44
Apiaceae or Umbelliferae Family 45
Plantaginaceae Family 46

Orchid Family 48

Rosacea Family 49

Tree Essences 51

Place Essences 52

Water Place Essences 52

44 Columbia River Gorge Flower Essences & Essences of Place .. 55

Angelica 57

Ball-head Waterleaf 59

Balsamroot 61

Barrett's Penstemon 65

Beacon Rock 69

Bleeding Heart 71

Buttercup 73

California Poppy 77

Camas 81

Catherine Creek Arch 85

Desert Sage 87

Fairy Slipper Orchid 91

Foxglove 95

Green Bog Orchid 99

Heart-leaf Buckwheat 103

Larkspur 107

Mock Orange 111

Moss 115

Mt Hood (Wy'east) 117

Mt Hood Lily 119

Mullein 123

Multnomah Falls 127

Ocean Spray 129

Oregon Grape	131
Oregon Oak	135
Phantom Orchid	139
Poet's Shooting Star	141
Ponderosa Pine	145
Pungent Desert Parsley	149
Queen Bead Lily	151
Red Columbine	155
Red-flowering Currant	159
Silky Lupine	163
The Columbia River	167
The Forest	169
Tiger Lily	171
Trillium	175
Wahclella Falls	179
Western Redcedar	181
Western Rhododendron	185
White Salmon River	187
Wild Rose	189
Willow	193
Yarrow	197
Affirmations of Wildflowers & Places	201
Glossary	203
Flower Essences and Elements	207
Flower Essences for Chakras	209
More Flower Essences	211
Acknowledgements & Gratitude	215
Camilla Blossom Bishop	217

Nature Awakenings

Years before I ventured into creating flower essences, I had an experience of meeting an aspect of my soul during a shamanic soul retrieval healing. A part of me was a gypsy. She was very lively, outspoken, and sensual and paid a dear price for using her voice. Her appearance felt important to me in understanding some of the fears and challenges I faced. I named her *Tangelica*. She became a part of me that I wanted to express and celebrate and heal. I brought her under my wing.

Flash forward fifteen years and I'm heading off to Tribal Bellydance class to have some fun and open my hips. I felt like a klutz the first class. I was dancing with a troupe of belly dancers that performed regularly and were young and lithe. I hadn't been dancing much so my body had forgotten the moves. But I felt called to sign up. The next class I remembered *Tangelica* and smiled. I realized that her name was magical. *Tangelica* was a combination of two flower essences I made: Tiger Lily + Angelica = *Tangelica*. I was floored! When her name came to me many years before, I had not made any flower essences, let alone flower essences from the two wildflowers that gave her a name.

Promptly, I began taking my new *Tangelica* formula of Angelica and Tiger Lily flower essences and attending Tribal Bellydance. I progressed, my hips opened, and my teacher asked if I wanted to perform. She said she'd help me get my costume ready. I wanted to dance but spirit was calling me on a journey. I left Hood River, Oregon for about four years on a sacred journey with a Native American elder to offer ceremony and healing to the spirit of water. I'll never forget the magical way these flower spirits showed up in my life to guide me to my future.

I began communicating with the spirit of nature as a child. Every spring the tulips and fragrant lilacs bloomed at my suburban home in Rochester, New York and reminded me of the joy of life. I'd nestle on my branch in the Magnolia tree as it flowered with miraculous blossoms. And, I grieved hard when our massive Elm tree was cut down. As summer warmed the landscape, I stayed outside and explored. Annual vacations to the forests of Big Moose Lake in The Adirondacks of New York allowed my happiness and imagination to soar. Even as a small child, I took walks in the forest by myself to enjoy peace and quiet. My heart bubbled with happiness at seeing wildflowers Indian Pipe and Trillium, playing with moss and Cedar, and swimming in the calm, clear lake. I was spiritually nourished by my relations with trees, plants, water, and sense of place.

Growing up, I excelled at arts and crafts, loved ballet and modern dance, played a clarinet, and enjoyed reading magical storybooks. I was very sensitive to energies in my environment but didn't know that at the time. It was very natural to feel the peaceful and healing energy of nature. As I grew up, I tried to move into the culture around me. As an empath, I was continually merging with my surroundings. This is a wonderful gift when you are in nature, but confusing when around others and in chaotic environments. I had no idea I was picking up on emotions, thoughts, and beliefs of my family, friends, and culture. It was hard to get a sense of self in the soup of my life.

I didn't have a clue how to navigate my changing body as I entered womanhood. I was a tomboy until I grew womanly curves overnight. In the late 1970s, feminism was the current form women's activism took and I became interested in women's rights quietly in my teens and then studied feminist theory and photography, among other things, at Ithaca College. I focused on my studies, activism, and social life that included the many joyful and difficult experiences of growing up. After college, I moved to Myers Point Park on Cayuga Lake with my boyfriend. Living by the lake lulled me back to myself. I remember standing in my backyard during the Harmonic Convergence in 1987. I knew little about this *New Age* event but had a moment of knowing there was something I was to do or be in this life and I needed to open to my Spirit to find it. I felt this calling since childhood. I didn't know what or how, but I knew a path was waiting for me. I walked in the Cottonwood forest by Cayuga Lake talking to my windsurfing friends about Edgar Cayce and enlightenment. We caught the breezes when the lake provided wind for our sails. A trip to Oregon with my windsurfing and skiing husband sealed our new life. We moved to Hood River in 1988.

Hood River awakened my love for nature, flowers, hiking, and love of surfing the windy waters and the snowy mountains. Windsurfing and snowboarding were spiritual experiences for me. Yet I was still seeking my place of belonging. My tribe. My journey into myself. Soon after arriving in Oregon, I had a very difficult time, I call a *dark-night-of-the-soul experience*, that set me on my course as a healer, herbalist, flower essence alchemist, and nature spirit alchemist. My husband and I lived in a beautiful new home we built in Hood River and had everything we could ever want. Yet, I was depressed. I began Hakomi Therapy, a body-oriented counseling therapy, to address my unhappiness. My soul was calling for help. Little by little, doors opened and set me on a course of personal healing, herbalism, flower essences, aromatherapy, numerous alternative healing trainings, spiritual initiations, shamanic teachings, ceremony, travels, and mystical and spiritual experiences that span decades. I continue to walk the path of a shaman and alchemist as my ancestors walked before me.

Oregon gave me a sense of place—a place I belonged. It offered a place to heal and develop my skills and learn to trust in myself, my imagination, my spiritual sight, and the spiritual realms. I began reclaiming my lost sense of worth and claiming my gift of being a highly sensitive empath—a gift than gave me my work. My commitment to walking the healer's path was strong even when it was painful. I felt I had made my choice; I was in the right place. Support surrounded me. Now, I needed to keep walking forward even when it was unclear where I was going.

My love affair with wildflowers, healing plants, and connecting with the fairies and the spirits of nature gathered energy on the Spring Equinox of 2000. I became a flower essence alchemist and went on to create hundreds of flower essences over the years and shared them with thousands of customers, clients, and students. I created a company to offer flower essences from regional Columbia River Gorge wildflowers and aromatherapy to bring healing on the emotional, mental, spiritual, and physical levels to others across the country. I taught flower essence alchemy to numerous students, healing practitioners, and apprentices. Many went on to create their own flower essences, open businesses, or use them in their healing practice or for self-care. The vibrational medicine from these Columbia River Gorge flowers, plants, trees, waters, and places want to be expressed in the world. They call me. The sweet wildflowers catalyze creativity and spirituality and teach self-love. Also, they want us to trust our intuition.

My work with the spirit of the flowers, waters, and lands awakened my memories—a remembering that my experiences are rooted in my past, my ancestral lineage, as well as the lineages of the First People's and ancestors of the lands. Before migrating to the United States, my ancestors cultivated relationships with nature spirits, fairies, Devas, and nature elementals. Fairies and nature elementals were part of my Celtic European ancestors' *religion*. Trees were our elders, ancestors, alphabet, and doorway to God's realms. Trees guarded sacred wells and were healers. Oak was considered the most sacred tree of all, *axis mundi*, the center of the world. This brought home a profound insight of my roots. Fairy medicine (Fairy Shamanism) carried in my DNA through my Celtic and Lemurian lineages allows me to energetically and intuitively connect with the earth's devic, fairy, and elemental realms. We know each other. I am able to receive and transmit nature's energies, healing, and messages. Much knowledge and wisdom is hidden in my own blood. My bloodline takes me far back into the ancient realms of alchemy, fairy and elemental shamanism, and Mother Earth herbal and indigenous and Grandmother traditions.

Through mystical experiences, I have connected with ancestors who are mystical fairy shaman, stone whisperers, Avalon priestesses, water priestesses, mermaids and water elementals, plant spirits, and even a petit fairy-like Irish woman of the mists. I've seen my lineage extend back to Africa, and I've connected with my elemental fire dragon and off-planet origins. My remembering takes me back to the origins of the earth and the Spirit Council of Thirteen Grandmothers. My ancestors are present with me now. My *Lemurian* Grandmothers guide me. *Lemuria* was an early civilization on the earth that celebrated water, nature, and the feminine will. My Ashkenazi Jewish heritage brings ancestral gifts in chemistry and alchemy.

My DNA continues to re-awaken, and remember, my origins. Over my life, I've learned much from traditional elders, shaman, Grandmothers, wise women, curanderos, priestesses, indigenous teachers, spiritual teachers, herbalists, and spiritual ancestors. I feel very grateful and blessed by these teachings and honor the ancestors that came before them. The elders help me remember the importance of traditions and how to cultivate our deep love and care of the earth. Also, I see how traditions emerge out of our ancient relationship with Mother Earth. Much of my practice flows from shamanic and intuitive and indigenous traditions that learn from direct personal experiences with the plants, waters, and earth. Most of my education comes directly from Nature and the spiritual realms.

I no longer run my original flower essence-aromatherapy company. I went on a sacred journey on behalf of water for several years. I returned with a desire to spend more time in nature instead of running my former business. After many adventures, I have spiraled back to the wildflowers continual love and presence in my life and continue to create and share flower essences and education at my home and through my website. My home, Prairie Star Meadows, is nestled in Pine-Oak woodlands surrounded by the beauty of native wildflowers, trees, waters, and magic.

This book feels like a song I sing with the flowers. It is born out of my personal relationship with the wildflowers, Devas, fairies, elementals, and ancestors of The Columbia River Gorge in Oregon and Washington. These wildflowers and places are very dear to me. Each flower holds amazing love, grace, kindness, and beauty. They have tenderly held my hand and my heart for many years as I have grown... and blossomed. And, they have compassionately nudged my *nature girl* within to play, laugh, and be vulnerable. When I allow myself to receive their love, I heal and expand with joy. These lands and waters have gifted me with a sense of place, a place I belong.

This book is a completely revised edition of *Listening to the Wildflowers: Guide to the Columbia River Gorge Flower Essences* (2008). I added new flowers, new discoveries, new wisdom, and emphasized the power of place and the sacredness of water. Enjoy the magic. All photographs and writings in this book are charged with the healing energy of nature and the wildflowers, elementals, Devas, fairies, angels, ancestors, and beings of light to help us activate our own relationship with the spirit of plants and places.

It is my hope that this book inspires others to develop their own relationships with the wildflowers and sacred lands. Nature's language of connection is through our heart and feelings. Through direct experience we learn and enjoy their precious beauty and consciousness. Be present. Listen. Spend time with them. Sing. Keep a journal. Be their student. Take their flower essences. Make flower essences. Open to the fairies, Devas, and nature spirits. Have fun. Fall in love with yourself and the plants, the places they live, and the waters that feeds us all.

*By loving these plants and flowers
you will know their deepest secrets*

*By loving yourself
you will know your deepest secrets*

Wildflowers are Calling

My first introduction to flower essences was through a friend sharing Bach's Rescue Remedy with me. Around 1990, I attended a day-long flower essence making workshop in Corbett, Oregon with Jane Bothell. My first flower essence, Quince, was made with a group of others. Joy Olson was my herbal teacher at the time. She created the *Klickitat Herbalist Guild* for our group of herbalists so we could gather periodically to wildcraft Stinging Nettle, Devil's Club, Elderberry, and other herbs to make medicine and our annual herbal cough medicine. It was a joyous time.

I was re-introduced to flower essences in 1994 after the birth of my son. The most beautiful day of my life as I welcomed my baby was also a profound and deep healing experience. Becoming a mother was a huge life passage. After the birth, I felt overly sensitive to everything. I couldn't be with other people or walk down the detergent aisle at Safeway because the smell was over-powering. I needed healing to repair and re-align my energy field. My body was going through an intense emotional releasing process. My nervous system needed support. At one point, I had a vision of my pelvic bones, covered with moss, floating away. My family suggested I take anti-depressants, but I knew I wanted to heal in a nature way. And, I wanted to keep nursing my son. Trying for a cure would only continue to suppress my emotions. I was very grateful to embrace herbs and vibrational energy healing. I began relying on herbal medicine, flower essences, aromatherapy, and homeopathy to nourish and heal myself during my struggle with postpartum depression and what felt like a nervous (system) breakdown.

Plants became my sacred medicine and life-line. Wildflowers and their flower essences helped me heal and made me happy. Energy healing and flower essences helped me express and release buried emotions and brought me back together. I delighted in the flower essence formulas my naturopath made. They seemed like magic. They helped me shift in amazing and gentle ways. I learned all I could about flower essences and their healing properties as I healed. I became a certified aromatherapist as well. I felt plants entering my life in strong ways, and they reconnected me to my ancient herbal roots and a new sense of community connection with other herbalists. Plants opened my world.

In 2000, I felt the spirits of the wildflowers in the Columbia River Gorge call me. In their subtle way, they called me. They asked me to create flower essences with them. So, two friends and I got in our car on the Spring Equinox and opened to the guidance of the flower Devas and guardian spirits. We felt a pull to go to a place overlooking Rowland Lake near Lyle, Washington. We approached with intention and asked *permission* to make flower essences as we walked the land. We found two beautiful wildflowers ready and willing. We placed glass bowls on the earth and filled them with water. We placed a flower in the water bowl and allowed the sun to transfer the wildflower's healing frequencies into the water.

When I began making these flower essences, a door opened wide in my heart to my true purpose. Connecting with the spirits of the wildflowers filled a deep longing within me. I felt blissful energy coursing through my body. The creation of the first two flower essences in the Columbia River Gorge—Grass Widow and Pungent Desert Parsley—was such a profound and moving experience that it awakened me to a deeply sustaining relationship with the spirit of the plants, Mother Earth, and the magical invisible realms of nature. I tapped into my gifts as an *alchemist*.

The lovely purple Grass Widow wildflower is one of the earliest blooming wildflower in the eastern Gorge and represents new beginnings. The flower survives severe weather. Its *medicine* (an indigenous and plant person's word for its healing gifts) gives us survival strength through greater self-reliance. I heard the plant say the word, "divorce." When going through loss of a relationship, we may suddenly feel like we are standing alone. The flower essence of Grass Widow can help. Pungent Desert Parsley has gentle deer medicine and warms our soul to help us express our true self. It is helpful for aligning the aura energetically when emotions or thoughts throw us off balance. This gentle, subtle plant spirit medicine helps us find balance especially if we are energetically sensitive.

Creating the Columbia River Gorge Flower Essences

Many of the Columbia River Gorge flower essences were first made in the spring of 2000 at the urging of the spirits of the plants. The three of us continued making flower essences through the spring and summer. Making the flower essences became my passion. We spent time meditating with the flower Devas and listening to their messages and talking about the flowers and plants and our experiences, observations, and intuitive feelings. We began taking the flower essences and sharing them with others. It was a wonderful way to learn about the flowers and build trust in our own direct experience. It was also fun, playful, and creative. I fully explored my imagination and the wonder of Nature.

Shortly after we completed making the first 84 flower essences, our three-way partnership shifted. Both women decided to move on. I asked the flower Devas and fairies if I needed to let go too. I wanted to find out if this was my best path. Less than a minute later, I could feel the energies of the flowers rushing back to me. They weren't going anywhere! We had just begun our relationship.

March 21, 2000 is the birthday of the Columbia River Gorge Flower Essences—at the turning of a new century. Each flower essence called to be created at a specific time and place in accordance with cosmic alignments. The glass bowls used for making the flower essences, and gemstone companions, were laid out on the Earth Mother in a ceremonial way that deeply honored the spirits of the land, waters, and elementals. Because they were made on the Spring Equinox using a Star of David sacred geometry, the essences hold the energy of balance. They hold balance of above/below, feminine/masculine, yin/yang, earth/spirit, heart/head and of the elements—fire, air, earth, water— with Love at the center. They were created with a sense of childlike wonder honoring magic and mystery.

I've been asked how I know the healing properties of the wildflowers. Grass Widow, Pungent Desert Parsley, and other wildflowers revealed their healing qualities through years of observation, meditating, taking the flower essence, in dreams, synchronicity, shamanic journeys, spiritual channeling, and intuitive ways. Students, clients, and apprentices shared their experiences in healing sessions, classes, and meditation circles. I learned from books, teachers, and flower essence colleagues. People showed up on my doorstep right after I created a flower essence they needed, and they shared their personal experience after using the flower essence. Also, I am an empath and clairsentient and have developed a strong intuitive nature as an energy healing practitioner. I sense and feel emotional energy moving through people's bodies in response to taking flower essences.

The Columbia River Gorge

Dramatic and sometimes steep cliffs up to 4,000 feet high run along each side of the beautiful river canyon along the Columbia River. The Gorge runs east-west about 80 miles along the big river which divides Oregon and Washington. Volcanic snow-capped mountains, including Mt. Hood (Wy'east), Mt. Adams (Pahto), and Mt. Saint Helens (Loowit), inspire awe through the seasons. World famous winds funnel and dance through the Gorge. There are many powerful places: natural stone arches, river canyons, unique basalt rock formations, hundreds of waterfalls, alpine meadows, towering fir forests, and pine-oak woodlands. Wildflowers grow everywhere. Elevation ranges from sea level to over 12,000 ft. Climate ranges from temperate rain forests in the west to arid desert grasslands in the east, creating incredible plant diversity.

The Columbia River Gorge deepens our relationship with nature's beauty and incredible potential. Geographically, the Columbia River Gorge formed from dramatic earth changes including extreme volcanic activity and cataclysmic flooding that cut deep walls into the lands during the Ice Age (Missoula Flood). Deep layering of the basalt rock formed a sacred geometric foundation of coherent energy covering this whole area. A coherent energy field is the same energy that radiates from an open heart.

Within its steep basalt walls and joyful waterfalls, The Gorge canyon gathers and contains potent healing energies. There is an abundance of

Devas, fairies, nature spirits, and earth elementals bringing joy and life-force to the whole area. The wildflowers of the Columbia River Gorge are imbued with sacred energy and with the knowledge of how to thrive with beauty and endurance despite the dynamics of extreme change. These wildflowers hold an untamed wildness and a way of being that reminds us of our own beauty and joy, like mirrors for the soul.

Flower essences created in the geologically dramatic Columbia River Gorge carry a very special energy of place. The wildflowers' medicine can teach us how to be open to our young and changeable nature, like the land. They are infused with the sacred beauty of the landscape, mountains, and rivers and waterfalls. Flower essences created here help us thrive despite cataclysm change, and teach us how to endure in challenging times.

Using flowers and plants growing in the same bio-region we live is sustainable and very healing. Our regional flower essences provide strong support for those who make their home here by providing a deepening of connection to this place and their sense of home. Taking these flower essences, or connecting to these plants, can also provide a perfect welcoming to those who have recently moved to the area to help them fully arrive, ground, and integrate into this geography, including newborn babies. Essences can help unwind patterns for those whose families or ancestors are from or passed through these lands or had some land connection in this area. If these essences are your medicine, you will feel an attraction to them or this region in Oregon and Washington. They combine well with flower essences from anywhere around the world.

Sacred Water

Water is our original medicine—it is life. Flower essences are a form of *water medicine*. Water carries the energy and intention of whatever we imbue it with on a vibrational level—what we put in water including thoughts, feelings, intentions, flowers, or substances will create crystallized patterns of consciousness. The water gathers the frequency of the vibration from the spirit of the plant—wildflower, tree, leaf that are placed in the bowl. The spiritual sound vibration of the flowers resonates seamlessly into the water. During a healing fair, a man approached my booth and told me he could *hear* all the songs of the flowers coming out of my flower essence formula bottles like exquisite symphonies of music.

I honor the water and water elementals when creating flower essences. I ask water to remember its origins and effervescence—flowing wild and full of air bubbles and passing along stones and logs and trees and plants against its bank. Wild water is happy water. When we take that in, we feel it on some level. Wild water can change our structure from within, and it nourishes our emotional body. I try to find pure, spring water when I can for this medicine as it is the vehicle for receiving the flowers, trees, and places.

In *Messages from Water*, and his other books, Japanese researcher Dr. Emoto photographed frozen water crystals to illustrate the way water carries energy and intention. He found loving thoughts, words, music created beautiful crystalline shapes when photographed. Discordant, imbalanced shapes were photographed from water exposed to pollution, hatred, anger. The photographs revealed the molecular structure of water as either beautiful or misshapen images depending on the intention towards the water. When flowers are soaked in water, they reveal beautiful symmetrical patterns.

The waters that feed the wildflowers of The Gorge become part of the medicine of the flower essences—the rain, snow, ice, and nearby creeks, rivers, waterfalls, lakes, and water sources. These magical places where the plants grow is overseen by water Devas and water elementals that bring effervescent life to the wild water. When we partake in an essence, the wild water speaks to our emotional feeling nature—our own inner-waters—in tones of joy.

Medicine of the Flowers

What are flower essences? Flower essences are an unscented water-based solution, a healing water, that is vibrational in nature and contains the healing Qi (life force imprint) of a flower, plant, tree, etc. They are made by placing flowers in a glass bowl of water in the sun, or moon, and allowing the Qi of the flower to be consciously transferred into the water by the radiating action of the sun. The water carries the flower's essence and is then preserved with brandy, glycerine, or vinegar to become a *Mother Essence*. Flower essences are considered vibrational medicine (ie, sound healing, crystals, homeopathy) and are commonly stored in glass dropper bottles.

Flower essences are most often taken by the drop in drinking water or under the tongue. I like to imagine them as drops of morning dew charged with the beauty and magic of Nature. No scent is captured with flower essences, yet they carry the flower's beautiful patterns of healing energy, Qi, in water. By taking flower essences, we receive healing frequencies that may be missing. They align our subtle energy system and help our body remember wholeness. The plants become our teachers and wise guides. With plants infusing our inner-waters, we become more trusting, compassionate, aligned with Nature's rhythms of balance and Mother Earth herself.

Historically, the essences of flowers were used for healing in Lemuria, ancient Egypt, Aborigines of Australia, Hildegard de Bingen (11th century Europe) and in shamanic traditions worldwide since ancient times. Some flower essences were created from morning dew while others received the healing affects by sitting with the plant and energetically receiving the flower vibrations. In the 1930s an English physician, Dr. Bach, re-introduced the public to flower essences. It is interesting to note that one of my teachers, Grandmother Maria Alice Campos Freire (a member of the *International Council of Thirteen Indigenous Grandmothers*), created floral remedies (flower essences) in the Amazon without any previous knowledge of them.

For times of transition, I find flower essences to be the perfect energetic tool to support us in finding balance and clearing old energies and patterns of stress that are surfacing to be released. Flowers hold a very refined, high frequency and potent life force—they are alive. Frequencies carried in essences are perfectly matched to reach higher levels of our subtle energy system to balance and clear blocks or congestion. The essences can naturally repair breaks in our electrical circuitry or turn channels of energy on where they have been switched off.

Flowers help us open our hearts. The light we take in from flower essences actually feeds and nourishes our nervous system and opens our evolutionary flowering process by harmonizing the relationship between our personality and true spiritual self. I believe flowers are keys. Keys that open our hearts.

Flower essences help us heal emotionally, mentally, and physically by addressing our higher spiritual frequencies, our deepest core emotions, and patterns (beliefs or habits) of imbalance that eventually crystalize, or already have manifested in the physical body. Flower essences offer us their unique support in easing the release of energetic blocks, unprocessed emotions, and patterns of beliefs. In order to blossom into our full beauty and potential, we must come to peace with our past including any childhood wounds—conscious or unconscious—and our ancestry. We cannot hold onto emotions without ill effect in our physical body. When we are supported and infused with healing frequencies of energy, our subtle energy system and chakras relax, ground out, balance, and flow with vibrant energy. New patterns of balance and health emerge from this process. They work beautifully in combination with all modalities of healing including medical treatments.

Taking flower essences opens us to nature's magic and communication with nature spirits, fairies, Devas, and elementals. My communication with the fairy realms and nature spirits has been strongly enhanced by using flower essences. They catalyze our ability to connect with nature and the spirit that animates the green realms. Working with flower essences personally, I've had many experiences of flower fairies entering my body to offer healing to my heart or places in my body that need love and healing life-force. My client, a massage therapist, reported seeing fairies for the first time when she started using flower essences in her practice.

The fairies looked like dancing sparkling lights on the patient's throat chakra. A yoga instructor saw auras that she doesn't normally see—beautiful green light coming from a healer's hands. Another woman started planting wildflowers around her house and began communicating with the flowers in new ways. She opened her heart to new friendships with flowers.

A flower represents the crowning moment of spiritual enlightenment of a plant. They help enlighten our bodies by raising the frequency of light we carry as they open us to new stages of our evolutionary ascension journey. Essences spiritualize our physical body as well as materialize our spiritual energy. They serve as bridges between the material and spiritual worlds and merge our higher self with our personality.

New alignment we receive from essences helps us rise above and ease release of old patterns of struggle around duality, polarity, and judgment. Flower essences help make change smoother and more integrated and supportive to all other healing modalities. Collectively and individually, we are freeing our soul of karma, imprints, emotional habits, and mental patterns that sink us into the old paradigm.

Flower essences are flowers of enlightenment because they raise the level of our vibration—our energy frequency. It is helpful to stay in higher frequencies to make it easier to create a positive outlook and more loving experiences in life. For healing and transformation, I find flower essences to be my miracle drops. Taking the essences of wildflowers activated my abilities as an intuitive energy healer, shamanic healer, and nature spirit alchemist. I need the flowers, and the flowers need me.

It always seems so magical to me that taking a few drops of water infused with flowers can calm my energy, balance my body, and even transform me in profound ways. It is as if the act of first taking these magical drops is an initiation in itself—into a world of our inner nature seeking full alignment with all of Nature! It is a simple and joyful way to care for ourselves, our families, our community.

The best way to truly understand this medicine is through our own direct experience of feeling or sensing them or observing changes in our attitude, behavior, health, or life over time. Learning to open to the flowers helps us learn to feel. *Feeling* is the *language of nature*. Communication with creation comes through the heart. After taking essences, some people have an immediate body sensation of feeling calmer, more grounded, or a stronger, cleaner flow of energy moving inside or around their body. Some experience profound energetic shifts, awakenings, or like to use them to journey into non-ordinary reality with the spirit of the plant. Others notice the effects when they forget to take them. Some feel deep joy and expansion or tears. For others, it may take weeks and a subtler sense of shifting or awakening of their awareness. It will also depend on our level of sensitivity and receptivity in the moment when we take them and the particular need being addressed as to how we experience them. All experiences are valid. We are forming a very subtle relationship with the plant. The plant, or place, is our healer and teacher and often work in unexpected ways.

As we emerge through portals of light into new ways of being and new ways of the Earth, we are learning new ways to stay centered, calm, and joyous! What the Hopi call the *Age of Flowers* is a new song for humanity. The doorway is now wide open into a new way of being, and walking on, Mother Earth. It is time for great miracles, synchronicity, and creativity. There is much space for love, freedom, and joy. Major changes are sweeping the Earth at this time for everyone. Massive healing is happening individually and collectively. This process of spiritual awakening—or human flowering—is unprecedented. Our bodies are changing, our minds are changing, and our whole beings are changing and becoming lighter. This ascension—Evolution Revolution—comes from within. Self-care is paramount. That is where our power lies, in the change, healing, and choices we make from within our own hearts.

Healing with Flower Essences

When do we need flower essences? Any time we are feeling a need for emotional, mental, spiritual, or physical support, taking a few drops of a flower essence or flower essence formula can soothe the nervous system and align our energy. Essences can instantly calm, support, and stabilize ourselves during crisis, illness, or injury or work more gradually as a truly holistic means for achieving long-term emotional or mental balance and deeper transformation. They can support personal healing processes, spiritual expansion, treatments, and surgery as they speed and ease healing recovery and assist in the integration of physical and energetic change. They can be very helpful in shifting our energy when feeling blocked, depressed, or negative. For spiritual expansion, flower essences can offer stabilization. Flower essences support a healthier perspective and our physical and spiritual healing process.

As Complementary Therapy

Flower essences bring beautiful integrated healing results when used in combination with other healing modalities. They move emotional, mental, or physical stress through the body for release. Therapies including chiropractic, acupuncture, energy work, massage or bodywork, counseling, breathwork, spiritual practices, meditation, shamanic healing, yoga, and medical treatments benefit greatly from the inclusion of flower essences. They will not interfere when used in conjunction with drugs and other treatments.

The healing process quickens because flower essences reconnect breaks in the optimal flow of energy within the nervous system. Healing shifts can be amplified and integrated into the body more quickly. Taking a few drops of flower essences during or after a chiropractic treatment, for example, helps the body hold positive new adjustments by assisting the nervous system with re-patterning and releasing of the emotional, mental, spiritual blocks surrounding a physical misalignment. It works by addressing and treating the core emotional cause for the imbalance, and helps assist the body in resolving the issue.

When facilitating an energy healing treatment, it is ideal to select the flower essences to be offered during treatment prior to the session. It helps open the doorway to receiving healing energy and also prepares the ground for any emotions or memories that may surface during the session. During a session, flower essences open awareness and shorten emotional processing time. After the session, flower essences stabilize, ground, and offer integration to the client. Offering an essence or formula blend for a client to take home helps reinforce the healing process.

Safety

One of the wonderful things about flower essences is their safety. They have no side effects. Flower essences work as needed and the essences that are not needed are simply released from the nervous system. Some may notice emotions and tears flowing more easily or body sensations that come with the circulation of energy in the body. Simply allow feelings to flow and they will pass. For very sensitive souls, the flower essences may bring what is called a *healing crisis* or the body's response to restoring balance. True healing may require a deep shift within the Soul, and the flower essences are working to support this shift. If the flower essence affects feel too strong, simply back off taking them. Those that are drawn to flowers for healing will benefit the most. Remember, healing is a process, there is no instant cure. Also, respect that some do not choose this form of medicine or way to heal. Flower essences are very safe for babies, children, pets, elders, plants, waterways, and the earth.

Flower Essence Therapy

Flower essence therapy is a form of healing that empowers us to incorporate greater self-care into our lives. When our focus broadens to encompass emotional and spiritual health, we expand our awareness to understand how our attitudes and thoughts can impact our health and happiness. And, from this place of fullness we can support our newborns, children, patients, animals, and Mother Earth by sharing this medicine. We can support and honor life's passages. Flower essences can be used in a celebratory way, to empower new life or a new season, to support our families, and expand our community of relations.

Children or Inner-Child

Children, and our inner-child, respond very quickly and well to the gentle calming effects of flower essences. Nature is the best balancer. Some children sense that flower essences will help them without needing any explanation. They are drawn to what they need. I've seen children become very energized and active initially after taking an essence. The flower essences align them so quickly; they feel great and want to dance and celebrate! I noticed this with my son and some of my client's children. One mother was a bit worried at the exuberant energy of her child. In a few hours, his energy leveled out.

*Flower Essences help your feelings flow like a waterfall
so they don't get stuck inside you.*

To engage our children in their own healing process, I ask them to choose their own flower essences. I show children photographs of the flowers or let them hold or feel the bottles. This gives the child a sense of power, and when they know we trust their intuition we are providing a beautiful gift to the child as well. Children are often much more open intuitively or psychically aware than we are, so they often have an innate sense of what they need. I made an essence for a recently adopted girl from China. She clutched her bottle and wouldn't let go because she was so happy to have what she needed to feel better. Another little girl calls the flower essences her *fairy drops*.

I add drops to water, juice, in bathwater, or a spray for their bedroom or around their body. Use flower essences as needed or 2-3 times a day. Select flower essences by dowsing, reading their description, or by using your intuition. Placing drops in their bath is an easy way to share the flowers.

Pregnancy, Birth, Postpartum Support

Taking flower essences is a wonderful natural way to prepare for pregnancy and to maintain balance and a calm presence during the many changes that take place during pregnancy, childbirth, and postpartum. In pregnancy, the flower essences easily reach and support the unborn child in addition to the mother. Test both mama and baby for essences. Pregnancy is a time of heightened sensitivity so it is important for mother to tune into the body, feelings, and outside influences to make good choices about self-care including what is energetically balancing. Flower essences enhance awareness and help bring emotional balance, mental clarity, and spiritual comfort.

Flower essences also work well right before and during childbirth to move through family patterns, resistance, and feelings of fear around birth. Baby and mama can be supported during the intensity of birth by testing for supportive flower essences during labor especially if labor stops progressing. They can help release emotions, stress, and fear and ease childbirth. For water birth, a few drops can be added to the birth pool water.

Birth is a key time to offer a beautiful *welcome* to a new baby soul with supportive flowers as it arrives on earth. A few drops can be applied to baby's forehead, in the bathwater, or to the hands as baby is held with love. After birth, newborns benefit from flower essences that their mother takes, especially if she is nursing. Drops can be added to bathwater to calm, balance, release birth trauma, and anchor the baby's soul more deeply in the physical body especially during the first six months. They can also address healing of birth trauma for baby or mother. Flower essences support parents during the postpartum period with the many changes that come with a new baby, a changing body, and new stage of life.

Energetically Sensitive People & Empaths
Flower essences are very stabilizing and clearing for those that are highly sensitive to energy. Many empathic and highly sensitive souls are drawn to the vibrational balancing and clearing energies of the essences, especially Yarrow, partly due to their ability to stabilize the nervous system during personal healing, environmental energies, earth changes, and ascension processes. Some *Sensitives* are better suited to using atomizers, placing the bottle on their bedside table, or to sit with the flowers for healing rather than taking them internally.

In addition, flower essences can be used to clear our auric field of energies and teach us how to maintain healthier boundaries and energetic integrity. Spraying ourselves, our space, or house clears the energies of emotions and thought patterns that may accumulate. Flowers are beautiful teachers and guides for sensitive souls. As an empath, I wouldn't want to be without them.

Pets and Animals
Dogs, cats, horses, and other animals are very responsive to flower essences for balancing and alignment. Essences are natural and safe. Pets need emotional balancing and are often very sensitive to the stress of humans and their environment. Add a few drops to water bowl, food, or apply to gums, ears, paws, or pet into fur. Use flower essences as needed or 2-3 times a day.

A woman with two alpha dogs who always pushed each other to go through the doorway first tried flower essences. Within days, the dogs stopped this jostling behavior. Some humans notice their animal's behavior change quickly while others see changes over time as pets become calmer or less needy. I recommend that humans also take flower essences at the same time to encourage more balance in the whole family system and the energy of home.

Land & Water
Flower essences are a beautiful *offering* or gift of gratitude for Mother Earth. Giving offerings is an ancient tradition that spans all cultures as it recognizes the importance of *gratitude* and giving back in a prayerful way. A simple ritual of sprinkling flower essences on land or in water is not only healing for the earth, it fulfills a sense of connection that is at the core of human longing.

The earth is made of energy and mirrors our own bodies. Placing specific frequencies of flower essences at places provides a powerful healing that can balance, clear, and harmonize land and water. Dowsing or using your intuition, select the essence(s) you wish to offer and sprinkle a few drops on the ground, on a tree, in the river or lake, or wherever you feel guided to place it. Add flower essences to water and land ceremonies or rituals. I have had direct experiences of strong elemental energy shifts happening when I have placed drops in different places and in bodies of water. In addition, I have had many profound experiences of inner-healing during times I gave offerings to the earth—the circle completes itself.

How to Take Flower Essences

My standard recommendation for administering flower essences is to take 3-6 drops under the tongue or in drinking water, three times a day for one lunar cycle or until you feel complete. For immediate need of stabilization due to a trauma, injury, emotional shock, stress, or transition, take them immediately and dose often. Take them as often as needed when past trauma is re-surfacing. If a *craving* for an essence is present, *saturate* the body by taking drops every half-hour or as needed. The body is asking for what it needs. Some take flower essences for several months to move through a healing process for chronic or deeper issues.

To be more specific, ask for intuitive guidance from the spirit of the flower or dowse using a pendulum or finger testing (see below) to determine the precise number of drops and for how long to take an essence. Or, simply take the number of drops that feel right. Notice if you aren't drawn to an essence anymore; that's an indication that you are complete. For some people, they may briefly circle back to an older remedy a few months later.

When taking flower essences, all healing is accelerating so you may notice healing quickening and shorter recovery times. Some people like to choose new flower essences daily or in the moment when an emotion or stress surfaces. This can be a powerful way to shift patterns—taking an essence to re-set habitual responses to a stressful situation when it is present.

Taking Drops Orally or in Drinking Water

Place 3-6 drops from the dropper bottle under the tongue (to reach nervous system quicker) or in drinking water. An easy way to remember taking flower essences is to add 3-6 drops to drinking water or a water bottle and drink throughout the day. Adding flower essence to water charges the water with the flower's healing energy and brings the medicine deep into our kidneys, the organ where fear is held. Flower essences can be routinely added to drinking water to enhance and amplify the water's frequency.

Bath Therapy
Another beautiful way to receive flower essence therapy is to add 3-6 drops to bathwater or a foot bath. Feel free to add essential oils and/or flowers with the flower essences. Soak in the sacred healing water and allow it to be received and absorbed. Make your bath a self-care ritual. Bathing in essences strengthens, repairs, and cleanses our protective aura; foot-baths bring in healing earth energy and support our grounding and the way we walk upon Earth Mother. Water offers deep soul purification.

Topical Application
Place drops directly on the skin on meridians, acupuncture points, chakras, sore muscles, or painful and congested areas. Some massage therapist place drops directly on tight muscles to relax them. Test which essences are best for specific issues or areas of the body. Add to lotion, oil, gel to use if desired.

Spraying/Atomizing
Atomizing flower essences around ourselves and our body's subtle energy field (aura) is a great option especially for very sensitive people. It is perfect for children and people in alcohol recovery and also to energize and clear a space and charge it with the energy of flowers. Use a feather fan to enhance the cleansing actions. Simply add 3-6 drops of any flower essence(s) to water in a mister bottle. The spray will last longer by adding some essential oils to the water as a preservative.

Saturating the Body
On beginning a new flower essence or formula, take drops of the essence often. Every few minutes, every ten minutes, every half hour for a period of time—a half-day, a full-day, or several days—to continuously saturate yourself in the frequencies. Saturation imbues your energy system to help set new patterns, awareness, and anchor new states of being. Do this especially if a craving for the essence is present. It means your body needs it.

In Recipes, Body-Care Products
Flower essences can be used in many creative ways. Add a few drops of any flower essence(s) to recipes, smoothies, juice, or herbal potions. Add to lotion, shampoo, soap, aromatherapy products, and other body-care products. Add in essences when you make your own body-care products.

Place drops on gemstones, in singing bowls, in water fountains, house plants, gardens, and wherever else calls to you. A former student who makes pottery added drops to her clay cups and bowls. I've added flower essences to paint. The vibrational energy of the flowers gifts all with their joy.

Sweeping Auric Field
Place a few drops on the palm of the hand and rub them together. After doing this, sweep the body's surrounding auric field with the hands with intention to cleanse and invigorate it. Use this technique when doing hands-on healing with yourself, adults, children, or animals. This works well for self-care and hands-on healers, for example, *Reiki* practitioners.

Tracing Meridians
For meridian balancing and cleansing, choose an essence for a specific meridian, apply it to the palms and take a few drops internally. Trace the meridian several times by running the palms a few inches above the meridian from beginning to end. (You can use a meridian chart.) Choose another essence for the next meridian. Tracing meridians according to the season can offer greater inner balance. (E.g., Trace the liver & gallbladder meridian during the spring and wood element.) California Poppy is a good overall meridian cleanser that can be taken and applied to the hands before Qi Gong, a Chinese movement that opens the flow of all the meridians. Acupuncturists can apply drops directly on the meridians or key points to open the flow of Qi in the body during treatments.

On Land & In Waterways
Placing drops on land and in waterways has a strong impact on aligning land and clearing congestion, human emotional fields, and distorted energy of earth ley lines (geopathic stress). The lands and waters are cleared, balanced, energized, and the nature elementals are nourished and fed by our offerings and gratitude.

Drums & Sacred Objects
Drops of flower essence can be rubbed into a drum skin or applied to a sacred object to infuse it with the plant's healing vibration.

Broadcasting
Do not underestimate the power of what I call *broadcasting* the flower essences and healing energies through our own body simply by taking them. When we take flower essences we become a vortex of healing that influences our family, loved ones, pets, patients, community, and Earth Mother. When we resonate with Nature, we bring peace and harmony to our world.

How to Select Flower Essences

Often the flower or plant we need most finds us—it tries to attract our attention—so when we ask with intention and then listen, we will find our medicine more easily. Try different ways of selecting and develop a way, or combination of ways, that works best for you. Here are some ways...

- Informational: reading and learning about the flowers and their healing properties; taking the essences to inform your body
- Observational: notice what flowers and plants are showing up everywhere you look; what flowers are now growing nearby?; did an essence bottle jump out of your hand, or fall off the shelf?
- Dowsing: using a pendulum, finger kinesiology, applied kinesiology
- Intuitive Meditation: meditate and hold a question in mind
- Dreams: ask for and receiving flowers and plants healers in your dreams
- Psychometry: run hands over the bottles to sense energy
- Knowing: guidance and awareness that happens without effort
- Clairvoyance: use visual stimulus like photos; observe auras around bottles; watch impact of holding an essence on a person's aura
- Clairaudience: listen to your guides or the spirit of the plants
- Clairsentience: sense or feel any energy shifts or sensations in the body
- *Sacred Spirit Deck*: pick cards from my oracle deck to select flowers intuitively

In general, a good way to select a flower essence is to start by bringing an intention into awareness. An intention may be: release stress and feel calmer; release my fear of failure; enhance my self-worth; be supported as a new mother; find help and guidance right now; transform old patterns; heal trauma; celebrate more joy. You can also hold an open intention of not knowing. The flowers that comes forward will reveal your inner-state.

For intuitive selecting, sit in meditation or quiet the mind and simply *ask* for an answer or guidance for the best flower essence. Be receptive and open. Let the answer come towards you—a picture, name, words, bottle, etc. Trust that first impulse or whatever pops in your head. That is your intuition! See what emerges: you may be drawn to a bottle, a flower appears in meditation, you hear a voice, you feel an urge to pass your palm over the bottles, or you start moving towards a photograph or plant in nature.

Practice makes it easier to select and builds confidence and ability. I use a combination of intuitive ways and dowsing to select flower essences. Dowsing is helpful because I have a large number of flower essences to select from. For some people, they prefer to learn the healing qualities of the flowers informationally or through using the essence and then selecting based on that information. Whatever way we are drawn to is the best way for us. We are all designed differently. The way we select may change as we grow and change.

There is no right or wrong choice. No matter which flower essence we choose, know that this flower has an innate intelligence. It will create a special relationship with whoever takes it, and it knows what to do. If we find a perfect match, transformation can be profound.

After taking flower essences, our ability to choose what we need, or what others need, strengthens. We learn about each flower or tree when we take their essence. Our body becomes a library of energetic plant knowledge. Shaman and medicine people store knowledge in their bodies and bones. Learning more about the flowers will open the channels of relationship and communication and soon there will be a stronger link.

I've created a full-color photographic *Sacred Spirit Deck* of the 44 flower and place essences in this book as an easy way to select flower essences. The cards can be used as *oracle cards* by holding them in your hands with the intention to select the flower(s) you need. Fan them out and pick one or more cards. They are amazingly accurate when used with intention and can be used to give flower essence readings and make formulas. Another way to use them is to look at the cards and see what flower jumps out.

Dowsing: Finger Testing & Using a Pendulum

For many people, dowsing with a pendulum, finger kinesiology, or muscle testing techniques are great methods for choosing the right essence, especially when selecting essences for others in a healing practice. We will focus on using a pendulum and finger testing here. Once we learn how to dowse, selecting is really quick and easy. Dowsing answers 'yes' and 'no' questions.

Finger Kinesiology/Finger Testing

This method uses our fingers to create a circuit or circle to show nervous system strength. A strong circuit with our fingers means the flower essence is strong and healing for us or our client. A weak circuit means it is not. Touch the tips of your left thumb and pinky finger together to make a circle—the circuit. Hold circle secure without straining or effort. Then, press the tips of your thumb and index fingers of your right hand lightly together and gently fit them upward into the circle you've made. Pulling apart gently the two fingers of your right hand, the circuit will hold when the answer to the question is yes. Test your circuit by saying: my name is _____(say your name). Fingers on left hand should hold steady—your circuit. Then say: my name is _____ (use a false name) and the circuit should break. Your circuit fingers will open. Adjust the level of effort you need to use to pull your fingers apart so you can test well.

Now, focus your attention on a flower essence, ask out loud, touch the top, or place the bottle in your lap and ask if the essence is strong. Try pulling out with your right fingers. If the circuit holds then the flower essence is good for you. If the circuit breaks and the fingers come open, then it's not strong. Switch hands if that is more comfortable.

Pendulum Dowsing

To use a pendulum, simply hold the pendulum in your hand suspended over your other palm and ask what a "yes" answer from the pendulum looks like; ask what a "no" answer looks like. Let the pendulum swing freely. Take note of which direction the pendulum swings for a "yes" and "no" answer. Then hold an essence in your hand (close to your body), hold the pendulum over the bottle, and ask the pendulum to indicate whether the essence is strong for you. If is swings in a "yes" direction, it will help you. Remember to hold trust in your answers. Doubt will interfere with good answers. When selecting for others, simply have them hold the bottle in their hand and dowse for them.

To test for groups of flower essences, hold a box of bottles, place them in your lap, point to them, touch them, or use your intention to make a connection to the bottles of flower essences as you dowse your "yes" or "no" questions. This can be done for lists of flower essences as well. "Do I need a flower essence that is present?" If you get a "yes" answer, test each bottle to narrow down your choice. You've selected the essences you need.

For testing others, hold a firm intention and make body contact with the person. "Does _____ (person's name) need a flower essence that is present?" If you get a "yes" answer, test each bottle to narrow down your choice.

When dowsing, it is important to make sure we are holding a strong intention and are clear and balanced before testing others for flower essences. Drink water, ground yourself, and balance your own energy especially if you are not getting accurate answers.

Creating a Flower Essence Formula

Flower essences can be taken one at a time or as a combination, or formula, using a number of different flower essences. This creates an alchemy of flowers, a new energy greater than its parts. Some choose to keep it simple by using 3-6 flower essences at a time. Others like to make more complex formulas with greater numbers of flower essences. I have created formulas using over one hundred essences holding very sacred intentions.

To create a formula, you'll need the *Mother Essence*, the original flower essence, or a stock essence. A stock essence is what you commonly buy at the store. It is made by adding 7 drops from the *Mother Essence* to a new bottle with water and brandy/vinegar/glycerine in a 1:1 ratio. To make a formula, simply add 3-7 drops of each flower essence to a clean glass dropper bottle with 1:1 spring water and brandy, glycerine, apple cider vinegar or shiso vinegar to preserve. Avoid touching the droppers to any surface to limit cross contamination of essences.

I like to create formulas very intentionally and *call in* the spirits of the flowers and plants to guide me. After creating a flower essence formula, I bless it by holding the bottle in my hands and ask my spirit guides and fairies and Devas of the flowers to marry and create a beautiful blending. Always, I thank the flowers for their medicine gifts. More and more, my formulas feel like living, changing, evolving beings that support our changing nature over time.

Preserving Flower Essences

Brandy is the traditional preservative for flower essences. For those who prefer to avoid alcohol, the *Mother Essence*, stock essences, and formulas (also called dosage bottles) can be created without alcohol. Alternatives for preservatives include glycerine, vinegar, and other kinds of self-preserving liquids like honey or programmable quartz crystals. In addition, flower essences made with brandy can be diluted in large quantities of water (E.g., a bath, a gallon jar of water, an atomizer) or added to boiling water to dissipate the alcohol present.

How to Make Flower Essences

Flower essences or vibrational essences can be created from seeds, flower blossoms, buds, leaves, pollen, roots, trees, bark, events, earth energies, crystals, waterfalls, and sacred places. Each part of the plant or place expresses a different quality of energy. Gemstone essences or gem elixirs are made in the same way (unless the mineral is unsafe to consume) and addresses issues relating to the crystalline and physical structuring of the body.

Making medicine with the spirit of nature is a joyous ceremony. I do not make flower essences because I can, I make them when I am called. The most powerful medicine comes through us in co-creation with Nature. Stepping out of the way in ceremony and honoring what is harmonious and healing is ideal. My essences are strong because I am co-creating and building relationships. I've received an invitation and their permission. It is more about making a place where The Creator can work… in this case a place for plants to be honored and medicine to be made from the flower and plant's subtle vibration realms—their consciousness. Plants are intelligent beings and wish to be treated as such by offering acknowledgement and gratitude.

These ideas come from my own experiences. Feel free to find your own way. Walk with intentionality in your life. I am often guided to get in my car and go to a specific place in nature. Then on the way I stop. Low and behold there are beauties awaiting me—the ones who have called. I have found many wild orchids, lilies, and brilliant flowers in these promptings.

For example, let's say you feel called to sit and receive healing from Peach blossoms in your back yard. You feel an urge to create medicine—a flower essence. The first thing I do is ask the Peach Deva (fairy or spirit or angel—whatever you want to call the spirit of the plant) for *permission*. Ask internally: "Do I have permission to make a flower essence of your flowers for my healing use?" Wait for a feeling, a rush of energy, a sense of truth, or an audible "yes". Feel free to use a pendulum or finger testing to determine your "yes" and "no." For clarity, it is best to be in a relaxed, attuned, and open state of being.

Before I make an essence, I often ask about timing. Ask the Peach Spirit when the ideal timing would be to co-create a flower essence. It may feel like "now" is the answer, or you may be given a sense of a day in the future or during a planetary alignment. Listen for the answers! Let yourself be guided, or use a pendulum to narrow it down.

I use a glass bowl without markings to make my essences. I make an *offering* to the place where I am guided to create the essence. Offerings can be a mixture of cornmeal, sacred water, a song, rose petals, lavender, or frankincense, etc.

I place the glass bowl under the plant or near the plant, or in some place that feels right. Before I fill the bowl with water, I like to sit with the plant and sing, drum, rattle, and/or meditate to align with the energies of the place and connect with the plant. There are many ways to do this. One way is to drop your attention into your heart space and breathe. Another is to breathe with the plant, filling your lungs with its fragrance and essence energy. Breathe in through the nose first. Then breathe in through the mouth. Breathe out as you offer your own essence energy. You can also make a circle with your breath by breathing into your own body and then breathing out and into the plant's body and then back to you again. Try this is one direction and then the other. You are blending your energy with the plant's energy. Singing, whistling, toning, drumming, dancing or movement, or meditation all can be effective ways to quiet the mind and open communication between yourself and the plant spirit realm. It's all about intention.

I fill the bowl with water from a pure water source or the best water I can find. Then I ask the plant Deva to make the flower essence medicine with me. You can state your intention and then you will get clearer direction as to what parts of the plant are called for in the flower essence making. Ask: "What part of you wants to be used to create this flower essence?" Open your awareness. Feel the plant's leaves, flowers, bark. Engage with it. Sing with it. Sense it. You may get a sense that there needs to be five blossoms and a little piece of bark in the bowl. Or you may be guided not to pick or gather any of the physical plant but dip the flower in the water without picking it. Go ahead and mindfully gather these items and place them in the water. Sometimes, I use a leaf or something so my hands don't touch the flowers. I don't like to use any metal tools or clippers because metal carries energy. Trust your intuition, your imagination, even if it doesn't feel clear. Do what feels good and true for you. The plant Devas can see your pure heart and intentions so there is no "wrong" way to make a flower essence.

I place the flowers in the bowl. You may also add sacred items, crystals, or stones around or in your bowl and make a beautiful altar. More than one plant can be made into an essence at the same time in the bowl. Ceremonies are times when we let the spiritual messages and guidance come through us. Let yourself be a conduit of the healing energies wanting to come through. Slow down and allow yourself to receive the medicine as you make it.

While the flowers are infusing their frequencies into the water, I meditate, make notes, observe what is transpiring around me and the medicine-making space or altar, listen for communication from Devas and elementals, relax, tune into my feelings, body sensations, visions, open to songs. Often, I hear songs I know. Sometimes, I've overheard human voices saying words that apply to the medicine of the plant. I keep my awareness open to the *language of nature* which comes through the heart as energy and vibration. Sometimes I am guided to leave the area for a time. Many times, animals or birds show up. Notice what happens before, during, and after the ceremony. There are many messages, signs, and wisdom coming to you in many different forms from the dimension of nature you entered. You are being shown clues to how the medicine is working with you.

When the flowers have been infused by the sun and the solar elementals (or moon) for a period of time, I often get a sense that the flower essence is done, complete. You can dowse to ask. The essence making process can take a ½ hour or ½ day or one day or overnight or several days. Then, I pour this water into a glass bottle and bring it back home. Before I leave, I make an offering back to the plant and Earth Mother using a portion of the essence-infused water, the *Mother Essence*, and give my gratitude. I also like to taste it and get a sense of its potency. I also make an offering of gratitude to the place with a song, love, prayer or appreciation. Plants are fed and nourished by our appreciation and gratitude. Please, say "Thank you!!!"

When I get back home, I strain out any small pieces of plant material, twigs or dust using an unbleached coffee filter. I add brandy (I clear its energy before use.) at a ratio of 1:1 (50% water/50% brandy). For a non-alcohol version, I use vegetable glycerine and water at the same ratio of 1:1. Some like to use vinegar 1:1. This is the *Mother Essence*. I like to succuss, or gently shake the bottle against my palm, to raise the potency until the *Mother Essence blooms*—there will be a sensation of the energy opening, flowering, or blooming. The *Mother Essence* can be bottled in canning jars, colored bottles, or any kind of glass container. It is best to store in a place away from EMFs, negative energy, or temperature extremes. I also ask, through a simple prayer, that my *Mother Essence* is stabilized and protected by light and love in eternity. You can take drops directly from the *Mother Essence* or make yourself a stock bottle by adding 7 drops to a new bottle. You are now a flower essence alchemist!

If you are going to share your flower essences with others, it is wise to consider this in your intention to co-create the flower essence medicine. This will allow it to be in resonance with others and not a medicine intended only for your own healing and alignment. Lunar essences are created in the same way as solar essences but carry a more reflective yin quality than from the sun. Floral waters are a simple way to get started. Place a flower from your garden (non-poisonous) in a glass of water and let it sit in the sunlight or moonlight. Drink the water or use in your bath.

Channeling & No-Pick Method

My relationship with the spirit of the plants and places and ability to channel and transmit energy has been used to channel flower and other essences. This process is done through meditation and intentional co-creating with the spiritual plant realms and allows the medicine to come through the ethers without being next to the plant.

My experience with channeled flower essences is that they work beautifully on the higher etheric realms and are especially good for those who are very energetically sensitive who are working with spiritual healing issues. In some cases, people working with issues that connect with the physical body are better served with a traditionally created flower essence. As our bodies evolve, our needs may change.

The *no-pick method* of making flower essences is a form of channeling an essence in the presence of the plant. A bowl of water may be placed next to the flower. You can make an essence without picking the plant either by dipping the flower in the water or channeling the essence. In the case of making essences from poisonous plants or rare and endangered flowers, the *no-pick method* and channeling are a must. (ie, Foxglove, Larkspur, Poison Oak)

Elements in the Wildflowers

Earth, Fire, Water, Air, Ethers in Flowers

All of Creation is born out of the elements of nature—Earth, Fire, Water, Air, Ether. The elementals create us and form our bodies and the bodies of plants. Plants carry a blending of the elements and, like us, some flowers express themselves with greater amounts of one or more of the elements of Earth, Fire, Water, Air. Learning about the elements is a way to understand a flower's healing nature and what may be elementally balancing for us. For example, we can take a fire-dominant flower essence to add more fire, balance our fire, or tame too much fire energy in our body. Or, we may take a water essence to balance, tame, or become aware of how we relate with our fire energy.

Plants dominant in Earth element help us enjoy our physical body and connect more deeply into the sensations of Mother Earth's body. They help us feel grounded. These plants and trees are stabilizing and earth-connecting like Oregon Oak, Heart-leaf Buckwheat, and Green Bog Orchid. They ask us to enjoy our senses and experience life by touching, feeling, dancing, singing, and enjoying form and its expression through manifestation in the material realms. We can release worry, dis-ease, and fears into earth. Earth elemental flowers and trees align us with the rhythm of the heartbeat of the earth in each of our moments. We learn how to nurture our dreams by tenderly *holding* them during gestation and growth and then *releasing* them into birth and then cycling through earth elementals *holding* and *releasing* again.

Fire plants carry a fiery spirit that may show up in their color, design, and love of heat and the sun. Some grow in the desert or drylands. Plants associated with fire include Balsamroot, Ponderosa Pine, and Oregon Grape. They are often yellow, orange, red, and love the sun. Yellow flowers are great for uplifting depression and infusing us with warmth and love. They fire up the sun of our third chakra. Fire plants embolden our spiritual forces and inspire our ability to transform like a phoenix rising. They are energizing and boost our creative life-force for more energy. If we need motivation, confidence, or willpower, fire elemental plants enlighten us with spirit and charge our solar plexus chakra for greater sense of personal power.

Water elemental plants like Trillium and other lilies, Western Redcedar, and Willow connect us with the emotional side of life and our intuitive feeling nature. Water plants align with our emotional body and give healing release to our grief, fear, and trauma so it can be resolved. Water is a healer. It softens our hearts and helps us feel safe in our vulnerability. It builds our self-worth by diving us deeper into our true nature where we can release and surrender into acceptance and love. Creation energy of birth and rebirth comes from nurturing womb waters—the mystery of life. We learn how to be more flexible, flow with forgiveness, set firmer boundaries (banks), and awaken our intuition. Water plants and places harmonize our hearts and offer their subtle balancing and healing gifts with grace and flow.

Angelica, Yarrow, Barrett's Penstemon are Air elemental flowers. Angelica and Yarrow have protective umbrella-like tops that reach into the sky. Yarrow's leaves look like feathers. Fragrant flowers are airy because their beautiful scent becomes air-born and we take in their healing qualities through our breath. Plants that have a strong response to breezes and the wind are air dominant. Barrett's Penstemon flowers grow high on the basalt cliffs of the Gorge where only birds dwell. Winged fairies are connected to this flower's medicine. Air elemental plants open all forms of communication including relationships with spirits, winged-ones, and ancestors. They move energy and bring delight in ideas, conversation, and mental activities. Mental clarity, communication, deeper awareness of the breath, and focus are supported with Air flowers. Air is an element of expansion, and fosters relationship connections.

When all the elements come together—earth, fire, water, air—into one, that is Ethers. The spirit of wholeness, health, and integration find home in Ether.

Flower Families

Plant Healing Signatures

Flowers are grouped together botanically in families to make identification and classification easier. Learning about a flower's family helps us to understand common healing themes and the *Doctrine of Signatures* as it is expressed in the plants. Understanding the *Doctrine of Signatures* reveals to us the way a plant can heal, whether by its shape, color, habitat, growth pattern, or gesture. It's all about patterns. Below are a few of the plant families represented.

Essences created from *flowers* address issues of our soul's evolution. Flowers address issues of creativity, sexuality, emotions and feelings, reproduction, enlightenment and spirituality, beauty, self-expression, purity, light, color, and sacred geometry. They teach us impermanence and spiritual communion. Wildflowers teach us survival and imbue us with their *wild* nature. Essences made from *budding flowers* or *small flowers* addresses development for babies, children, inner-children, and the inner-birthing process. Under-developed aspects can be seen and met with flower buds. Essences of *seeds* address creation energy, ancestry, potential, origins, fertility, conception, new life, growth, birth, and rebirth.

Lily Family
Rebirthing & Reclaiming the Sacred Feminine
Element: Water

As soul medicine for our Spirit, the gentle Lily Family addresses issues of the feminine and women's worth: creativity, purity, beauty, spiritual sensitivity, sexuality, motherhood, birth, rebirth, grounding, embodiment, receptivity, compassion, and love. Lily flower essences can also transform the emotions (especially grief) or traumas that are held in women's and men's bodies that effect their cycles, organs, and health.

The number 3 is significant to the lilies as their parts (petals, sepals) always express in multiples of three. In numerology, 3 is a creativity, birth, and communication number.

The first message I heard from the lilies was: "Lilies give women permission to be women." Years later, Tiger Lily shouted, "Create! Women. Create!" (see Tiger Lily)

All lilies bring joyful celebration and the energy of compassion. Lily flower essences offer women, and the inner-feminine within men, a portal to a gentler, more loving, and compassionate way of being as well as a guide to the life of the divine. The very pure and high frequencies of the lily flowers can nudge outdated belief structures and are especially helpful for very sensitive and feminine souls. Many experience lily essences as bringing a celebratory delight to their delicate sensing and feeling nature and a strong sense of recognizing their own personal energetic space, or boundary, sometimes for the first time.

On a physical level, a woman's reproductive system may be supported and balanced with lily flower essences by addressing the root emotional causes, beliefs, and spiritual inheritance. They help dislodge the emotion of grief from the body. The medicine of lily essences offers a gentle, safe, and natural fluidity that addresses blockages and imbalances in the body—PMS, infertility, menopausal symptoms, and congested or stagnant Qi in the pelvic region.

Like the lily flower, lily-type women, or men, can feel shallowly rooted in the earth. They can be very energetically sensitive and emotional with a pure spiritual nature. It is best for them to avoid extremes and be in situations that help them feel safe. Taking flower essences from lilies can enhance a sense of self-worth and personal boundaries and helps us honor the importance of self-care.

All the lily flower essences in this book were created from wild lilies growing in the Columbia River Gorge. These lilies are untamed—wild and free. Most of the year, their essence is stored in a watery bulb underground. After a short blooming, they retreat back into the earth and are reborn again the next spring. To me, lily flower essences are sacred waters of the feminine, honoring the beauty of our feeling nature and creative-sexual feminine power.

The white lilies called to me as I was exploring my essential innocence and pure feminine spirit. White carries all colors. It is the color of pure spiritual light, our connection to the divine, and of love of a giving nature. White purifies and softly awakens our gentle and subtle nature. This gentle softness is so desperately needed on Earth. The purity of the white lilies helps erase the judgement of shame and guilt women have carried simply because they are women. White lilies re-birth our feminine nature, bodies, and sexuality regardless of our ancestry, past, or what experiences our bodies have encountered.

> *"In my vision, I saw a Great Pyramid of stone
> and from it emerges a giant White Lily.
> As it gently blooms, the pyramid crumbled."*
> —Helene

In this time of the "passing of the torch" to the feminine, Helene's vision feels like a perfect metaphor of the symbolic rebirth of the divine feminine amidst the crumbling of old structures, i.e., patriarchy.

> *"I first took White Lilies [Essence formula] at a workshop led by Camilla where we were learning how to connect to our ovarian energy. We took a journey with white lily essence and I felt deep feminine, mermaid, and tree energy. I was transported into my womb space and it felt like a new celebration of the womb occurred within me. I am home, I felt. My ovaries began to speak to me. I knew my sensual self more deeply. Months later, I put White Lilies Essence in my bath and meditated with the goddess Venus. Venus taught me it is okay to take time to luxuriate and beautify myself. She taught me that I could surrender to my femininity. Taking this essence has also brought many opportunities into my path to heal my second chakra and relationship to sex."*
> *— Elyssa*

Ball-head Cluster Lily, Camas, Chocolate Lily, Glacier Lily, Green-banded Mariposa Lily, Mt. Hood Lily, Tiger Lily, Trillium, Queen Bead Lily.

Asteraceae or Composite Family
Balanced Masculine Warmth & Confidence
Element: Fire

The Asteraceae or Composite Family flowers are actually one flower made up of many hundreds of little flowers in some cases. Each flower has disk and/or ray flowers within its complex geometry. The composites have strong and hearty physical presence and are very stabilizing and grounding. They are considered some of the most evolved flowers on Earth with a strengthening nature. *Aster* means *star* in Greek. These flowers represent wholeness.

As water is to the lily; fire is to the composite flowers. Associated with the Sun, the composite flowers bring us solar warmth and life and encourage differentiation. The fire plants bring us a flame of self-awareness, self-determination, heart connection to give and receive love, and the purification energy of a phoenix rebirth. Composites offer the Sun's transmuting energy.

The light of the Sun in these flowers is a nourishing food that helps us grow. The Sun's energy holds the healthy masculine qualities we all need—spiritualized ego, higher wisdom, spiritual leadership and knowledge. We can learn to balance our personal will with the greater solar will. The solar masculine energy helps us feel radiant and confident. This is what we need our fathers to teach us. Composites call back many hundreds of flowers into one unified force, like the sun.

Balsamroot is like the *Sunflower of The Gorge* and grows all over the sunny hills in the eastern Gorge. Its roots grow very deep; it is well established. It offers us an important male elder teacher, Grandfather. It can be used for adolescent boys and girls to develop confidence and maturity and for adults to spiritualize their ego forces and support their leadership potential.

Yarrow is a universal healing plant, growing worldwide to offer its important protective medicine for vulnerability and a stronger sense of wholeness.

Balsamroot, Dandelion, Marigold, Pink Yarrow, Yarrow.

Apiaceae or Umbelliferae Family
Sensory Integration, Gentle Protection & Channel for Spiritual Light
Element: Air

The expansive and radiant Apiaceae or Umbellifereae Family flowers are like umbrellas of protection. Gently offering their shelter when we feel vulnerable or need rest or stillness. Their well moistened roots grow into airy flowers with spokes of an umbel that radiate out from one single point. Their leaves and flowering patterns suggest a connection to the nervous system and a way to enhance integration and soothe stress-related issues. In part, the integration of sensory input is beneficially affected, for example: over-stimulation, hypersensitivity, nervous breakdowns.

Those with hollow stalks move energy and open us to being conduits of life-force and earth energy. We remember our purpose as open channels for divine and earth light through our flexible liquid crystalline bodies. We can tune and receive and respond to the light available with awareness. They help us transmute change by breathing more deeply into our roots.

Apiaceae Family (also called the celery, carrot or parsley family) flowers also purify our body electric—moving and cleansing the energy flows and channels. Many plants are edible but some are highly poisonous (Poison Hemlock)—know your plants! Many herbalists steer away from teaching about the Parsley plants because some are so toxic, but I have always been very attracted to the native parsley flowers of The Gorge especially as flower essences. Some of them are used for food or ceremony by indigenous people of the Pacific Northwest. Fern-leaf Desert Parsley, *Lomatium disectum*, is highly regarded as an herbal medicine and reputed to be used successfully during deadly flu epidemics.

Angelica, Cow Parsnip, Pungent Desert Parsley, Queen Anne's Lace.

Plantaginaceae Family
Freedom is the Word; Courage is the Way
Element: Air, Fire

The Devas of the Plantaginaceae Family of plants (Penstemons, Foxglove) are very sweet and joyful. They tell us, "Drop the fear and move into love. It is time to play." Freedom is what they teach. Being responsible for ourselves is how we become free. Respond by taking action steps towards what we desire.

Penstemon and Foxglove flowers have a tubular shape that opens wide at its mouth as if it is ready to open and speak. The ones I have found in the wilds are usually beautiful shades of pink, purple, or reddish in color; white and purple for Foxglove. *Penstemon* means *five stamens*—the male part of the plant—and brings the strengthening aspects of masculine action.

"We want humans to be happy
We want you to be without doubt
Your courage lies within you at all times
Your courage is about freedom
To feel and own joy
By standing up for what and who you believe in"

These penstemons encourage us to take action, even in a small way, to show our conviction to move through fears collected in the root chakra. Our commitment to life will be seen, and the Universe will rise to meet us.

Penstemons are excellent universal flowers to cover a wide range of psychological issues including social anxiety, phobias, fears, and unknown or undiagnosed issues especially related to the root chakra—childhood issues, inheritance, security issues. The native wildflower Barrett's Penstemon is endemic to Oregon and Washington. It addresses fear and trust issues and helps us move towards joy.

At one point, I was called by the penstemon flowers to create their flower essences. They told me telepathically to put different penstemon flowers together to make a formula to help humans with fear. I was busy so I didn't do it. During a walk at Horsethief Butte a few months later, I began scrambling up the rocks of the north face. Soon I was overcome with a horrible fear in my gut. I don't usually have such an intense experience especially out in nature. In that moment, I spotted a beautiful penstemon. I stood before the plant and spoke: "Ok, I'm listening now. You told me to create a formula of penstemons for fear. I get it!" I created the formula and it became a very popular flower essence blend that addressed all forms of psychological issues including fear. One woman was able to avoid using antidepressants because it worked so well to elevate her moods. She loved that the medicine was safe, natural, and non-addicting.

Foxglove brings us freedom through the courage to move inward towards the heart of emotional honesty and vulnerability.

Barrett's Penstemon, Foxglove.

Orchid Family
Evolutionary Catalysts, Activators of Truth, & Venusian Masculine Awareness
Element: Water

In ancient times, orchids were an important ingredient in love potions and a fertility symbol and aphrodisiac. Originally, the orchids told me their flower origins were *Venusian* so I assumed they were carrying the feminine healing frequencies (yin). Then I had a corrective dream. I saw a huge glass case of different kinds of orchids on display. When I stepped closer, I realized they were all penises. The orchids are holding potent masculine healing energy. In my research, I found *orchis* is Latin for *testes*. I adjusted my gender bias with the wild orchids and embraced their lovely masculine/yang healing energy from Venus.

Orchids are for the timid. Orchids lead us to the light within—the part of us often feared more than our darkness. Orchids catalyze truth. They move us beyond our illusions and denial. Spending time with them, I sense them saying:

> *"Dare to express yourself, dare to experience your sexuality, dare to enjoy abundance and pleasure, dare to free your moral and social conditioning, dare to celebrate your spiritual power."*

Orchids have also been associated with wealth, greed, and lust. Considering orchids' evolutionary status, it may seem contradictory that orchids bring this out in people. I see this as a natural evolutionary process of being led through our ignorance, or lack of awareness, in order to become wise. I feel the orchids are leading us on a journey, clearing our illusions, blind spots, shadows, and darkness. They ask us to recognize any restriction or repression of our natural impulses.

Orchids are a rapidly evolving flower and are potent activators for our own evolutionary process, including opening our psychic gifts and raising our energy frequencies. Orchid essences push us through our blocks and fears. They catalyze change and transmute whatever truth is being denied. I find orchid essences strong and assertive in their actions. They move self-limiting beliefs out of the way and lessen the power of fear by focusing on optimism and strength.

Also, orchids ground us in earthly sensual life. They help release karmic patterns and long-held emotions, and they open us to receptivity and the joys of being human—touch, intimacy, pleasure, sensuality, and eroticism. Orchids balance the masculine and feminine within and bring greater trust so we can surrender. They spiritualize our sexuality and can awaken kundalini with a focus on the heart. Orchids open us to deeper union.

I had no idea there were so many different wild orchids in the forests of Oregon and Washington. I find them everywhere. Phantom Orchid appeared like a lantern in the dark woods, a mysterious beauty. He told me what his medicine was about *illusion*. Coralroot orchids, White and Green Bog Orchids, Phantom Orchid, and Fairy Slipper have strong and varying personalities. I am really intrigued with their energy as agents of truth and our ascension process of moving beyond illusion.

Fairy Slipper Orchid, Green Bog Orchid, Phantom Orchid.

Rosacea Family
Love & Heart Healing
Element: Earth

Roses bring love and compassion to humanity and heal the depths of a tender heart. They open and connect our heart to greater unconditional love, divine love, romantic love, faith, devotion, and our true spiritual nature. The highest frequency of any flower, roses intoxicate us with their beauty, colors, scents, and symphony of songs. Love songs, poetry, and the finest perfumes sing with the magic of the rose. As an aphrodisiac, rose is the flower of romance. Roses love lovers, and they help us trust in love again.

Venus, The Cupids, Aphrodite, and the Rose Queen encourage us to experience fulfilled, liberated partnerships. Rose flower essences encourage our heart to grow and blossom with new ways of love that are unconditional and spacious. We learn to feel safe and re-open our hearts again to new people and circumstances. They heal the heart deeply and to the core. Those who retreat because they have been hurt, battered, or betrayed when trying to love need the tender caresses of roses. When our bodies get stuck in resentment, anger, or hurts of the past, try roses.

Rose flower essences are very powerful for integrating energy shifts and grounding new energies especially through the nervous system, sacrum, brain, heart, and cerebral spinal fluid (cranial-sacral therapy). They fill us with love and feed our nervous system with loving moisture.

When apathy sets in, roses can instill passion for life. Their energy is very heart-centered and expansive. All Rose Family flowers feed and nourish our energy system through the heart center.

Roses were made for humanity. Roses have five petals. Humanity's number is five—for our five fingers and five toes. The thorns remind us that life carries hurts, snags, tears, but we must accept the thorns as well as the deep, rich beauty of the flowers. The thorns can actually protect our sensitive hearts. Roses support us as we incarnate in our body and help us receive new spiritual energies. The Divine Feminine, Mother Mary, and Goddess energy are deeply connected with the rose. Also, red and white roses connect us with the fairy realms.

Apple Tree, Broad-petal Strawberry, Hawthorne Tree, Ocean Spray, Wild Rose.

Tree Essences

Essences made from *trees* address issues of strength, endurance, grounding, guardianship and the conduit between heaven and earth—*Tree of Life*. Tree are our ancestors, guardians, teachers, elders, and gatekeepers into the Fairy realms. To the Celts, trees were their alphabet, the *Ogham*. Oak was the *Tree of Life*, *axis mundi*, center of the world, and door to the *Otherworld*. The trunk of the tree represents the center, backbone, consciousness, and relationship to gravity and our *central channel* or core essence. Essences made with *roots* represent our foundation, ancestry, structure, and what is hidden from view, nourishing, and deep within. Essences including *bark* offers protection, insulation, and a form of energetic boundary. *Leaves* are the breath, or respiration, of a plant. Protection, strength, communication, and sunlight nourishment come through leaves. *Needles* and *catkins* are antennae, receptors, communicators, and protectors. *Fallen leaves* help the surrendering and letting go process. *Flowers* are the highest evolution of the plant and they bloom with creative-spiritual expression. *Fruit* essence provides energetic nourishment and renewal as food for the energy body. A fruiting tree represents joy and how to generously share our gifts in service to all of Creation.

Trees carry ancient wisdom of the earth as earth-keepers. Trees are channels of life-force and earth energy and carry a strong earth elemental energy. They ground us in the earth with their roots and connect us to the divine with their branches. Trees help us become conduits of light to connect heaven and earth. The *Tree of Life* is a cross-cultural symbol that represents the interconnectedness of all life on earth. As lungs for our planet, trees spread amazing love and strength and breath for the whole earth. Trees are strengthening, supportive, and present. In an intuitive message from Western Redcedar, it asks that each one of us become a *Tree of Life* too. Ponderosa Pine gives us peace and asks for our peace in return. Oak wants us to yield to its strength and open the door to the *Otherworld*. Trees balance humanity and breathe *with* us.

Ponderosa Pine, Western Redcedar, Willow

Place Essences

Sacred places connect us to the spirit of Mother Earth and the ancient ancestors that live there. Each place holds its own sacred medicine and energy and can be honored for its beautiful wholeness. We are gifted with overflowing healing when we touch these place with our walk, songs, offerings, and reverence. Our generosity and gratitude feeds and nurtures the spirits of nature of the lands and waters. We make places stronger; they make our hearts stronger. Place essences bring the healing energy of a place directly to us—that special frequency created by the elemental combination of nature's exalted joy and purpose.

Essences made at *places* offer us a sense of place, a sense of belonging. They connect us to the land and Mother Earth. Access to healing earth energy is enhanced, and we inform our bodies through the land's healing imprints. Place essences enhance the relationships we have with the spirits of the land whether that is nature spirits or ancestors, stone, plants, birds or animals. Places can be healing, restorative, balancing, cleansing, and initiatory.

Beacon Rock, Catherine Creek Arch, Mt. Hood (Wy'east), The Forest

Water Place Essences

Being in water places washes us with restorative, blissful, sensual, healing light and aligns our emotional and feminine nature. The spirits of water delight in healing and communicating with humans. They love our songs. The language mermaids, water elementals, water dragons-serpents, Devas, water babies, and Salmon speak is a heart language—feelings and emotions. Our being nature is nurtured in water places. We learn to honor our innate flow, the cycles and rhythms of our lives, and how we heal from this place of simply being our essential self. Indigenous people say, "Water is the original medicine."

Water essences connect us with the element of water and the elemental beings that enhance flow, fluidity, movement, and dreams. Water cleanses us, heals us, and supports our emotional and feeling nature. Water elementals speak in sensual, joyful, freeing ways to awaken the delight of our feminine intuitive gifts. Water essences help us see nature's mirrors so we will claim our own watery nature and our heart's desires.

Multnomah Falls, The Columbia River, The White Salmon River, Wahclella Falls

44 Columbia River Gorge Flower Essences & Essences of Place

It's time to meet the wildflowers and places that carry the sacred spirit of The Gorge! Open and receive their healing energy frequencies from these pages. Take or make the flower essence. Here's a chance to enter new and deeper relationships with these plants and places.

The *plant spirit medicine* and *nature spirit medicine* are available to anyone at anytime from anywhere. Without access to these wildflowers or flower essences, connect to the spirit of plants and land with intention. Connect to the plants, places, and waters where you live. Make flower essences with them. Being in nature, gardening, making altars, doing nature ritual and ceremony, working with land, sitting in meditation, doing spiritual practices, shamanic journeying, giving prayers and offerings, singing to waters, and asking for relationship intentionally opens connection and communication with the spirit of plants and nature.

Please note that flower essence therapy is not intended to take the place of medical diagnosis or treatment. If you have health concerns, please visit a healthcare provider. Taking flower essences is a supportive complement to any healthcare treatment.

Angelica

Angelica genuflexa
Affirmation of the Wildflower: "I am an Earth Angel"
Element: Air, Earth

Anxiety • Channeling • Compassion • Death/Dying • Detoxification • Epilepsy • Fatigue • Hypnotherapy • Illness • Intuition • Meditation • Nervous System • Nourishment • Patience • Protection • Purification • Receptivity • Self-discipline • Sensitivity • Sound Healing • Stress • Support • Surrender • Trauma • Vision Quest • Vulnerability • Chakra 7 (crown)

Balanced: open channel to angelic guidance and divine light

Angelica grows to reach the Heavens. Its spirit can help open an inner sense of spiritual or angelic light and help you know that you are protected and connected to spiritual assistance always.

Angelica is a gently protective wildflower with an umbrella-like shape. At the same time, it's creamy white flowers radiate upward towards the light of unconditional love—*Christ Consciousness*. Parsley flowers are supportive of integration in the nervous system and for integration of sensory input—calming hypersensitivity and feelings of vulnerability. The stalk is hollow offering a perfect open channel for pure white light and higher frequencies to be received... and given.

In *Flower Essences and Vibrational Healing*, Gurudas channels that Angelica was developed to counter-act stress related illnesses for sensitive souls. It can assist in autism by bonding together diverse parts of the personality. Angelica is excellent for meditation and psychotherapy. In the latter case, it "provides intellectual or rational information to resolve the issue." Because of its effect on the nervous system, epilepsy can be treated with Angelica. Its essence is useful in hypnotherapy as well.

I have spent time with Angelica and whales on the coast of Oregon, on

Mt. Hood at Lost Lake, and near Multnomah Falls. One November, my friend Angela found a fully blooming native Angelica flower near my home. All the other plants were blackened by freeze or dieback. In numerology, 11 11 is a master number signifying that angelic communication is present and real. Pay attention. *Angela* found the *Angelica* on 11/11, the day of *Angels*. It felt like an angelic sign; I needed to make this essence. I made the Angelica flower essence on 11/11/2009 (2 + 9 = 11). I let the flower gather the solar energy at 11:11 in the morning.

The flower essence feels very expansive and light-filled and *angelic* like its name. It was reminding me how to be an Earth Angel and bring my angelic nature to the Earth. Earth Angels, like real angels, heal by their presence and will not try to *fix*, interfere, or give advice unless asked. This angelic way is the new paradigm healer's role.

Angelica flower essence can have an immediate effect of aligning people with their higher light. I offered the Angelica flower essence to people at the first *Portland Plant Medicine Gathering*. Their faces and crown chakras lit up as soon as they took it—their *lights* switched-on and their angelic nature awakened right before my eyes.

• Scott wrote, "I am a hands-in-the-dirt, plant medicine kind of guy, and though I love the idea of flower essences, I rarely work with them. Camilla offered me some of her Angelica 11:11 essence to try at an herbal gathering. As soon as I took the drops I felt my crown open up and intense energy began flowing in from above, raising me up. I had to really fight to stay centered and within myself as I was awash with heavenly energies and surrounded by beings from the heavenly realms. It was quite an experience that left me with a clarity and focus that I associate with encounters with beings of light from above."

• After taking Angelica, Chris, a social worker, said he felt unusually clear, helpful, and steady with his long line of clients on the night shift. He was able to be a steady presence while being in a more fatigued state than usual. Perhaps he appeared as an Angel to many of his clients that night.

Meet Angelica at Multnomah Falls or Latourell Falls in July.

Ball-head Waterleaf
Hydrophyllum capitatum var. thompsonii
Affirmation of the Wildflower: "I open to the flow of life"
Element: Water, Air

Certainty • Clarity • Divine Guidance • Fear • Focus • Headaches • Head Congestion • Individuality • Inspiration • Mental Balance • Over-thinking • Self-assertiveness • Self-worth • Spiritual Identity • Trust • Will • Chakra 3 (solar plexus), 7 (crown)

Balance: flowing energy in the crown and head area brings clarity of thought and divine inspiration

The ball-shaped flower-head blooms in all directions like an expanding mind. Ball-head Waterleaf stimulates the flow of energy in the crown of your head and activates the potential for new forms of inspiration.

Ball-head Waterleaf grows under the Oregon Oak trees in the Pine-Oak Woodlands of Oregon and Washington. It's fun to see the flower before it blooms because it looks like an orb—a compact green ball—sitting on its stem. Visiting the flower as it blooms reveals a new sense of wonder as numerous pale lavender-colored florets shape a newly expanded flowering head. It reminds me of what an open-mind looks and feels like as it expands: clear, trusting, certain and beautiful. Its shape has shown up during a healing vision as a multifaceted diamond with each face (floret) representing a different archetypal expression. A sense of wholeness comes with the integration of all our aspects.

The spirit of the plant told me it opens us to the *Wisdom of the Ages* and helps us access our personal spiritual energy. It opens the energy at our crown chakra at the top of our head so we feel connected. It brings more openness, spaciousness, and trust in the Universe and a Higher Power. Keeping an open mind allows a willingness to experience, notice, and believe new thoughts. Openness allows us to receive higher guidance and access our *knowing*.

Ball-head Waterleaf works well in moving congested head energy. Energies like thought forms, ideas, or beliefs can get trapped around the top of our head. For example, someone with a headache or a very logical person who tends to lead with their head, as opposed to their heart, would benefit from this flower essence. The flower can bring more clarity and enhance the flow of energy in and around the head. The leaves are called *waterleaf,* a reminder to allow thoughts to flow like water. This increased flow assists us in bringing our awareness deeper into our body and our heart space. It enhances our spiritual identity and helps us focus and strengthen our intentions.

• R.H. wrote, "After my son's death in 1995, I had developed a mental pattern of attempting to read through circumstances of his unexpected death, never successfully commanding an answer. Within two days of my beginning use of Ball-head Waterleaf I experienced quite a sudden mental and physical elimination of congested patterns. Less than a month later, I can stand free of repeating my mental repetitions of a problem and truly experience my central spiritual clarity."

• Jannine wrote, "I can tell you for a fact, that Ball-head Waterleaf quickly became the first thing I reach for when I feel a headache coming on. I run a lot of energy doing massage and my work as a college Dean, and energy often becomes stuck in my head. Ball-head Waterleaf seems to help clear and open the stuck, constricting pressure I feel so that the headache lessens and often leaves."

Meet Ball-head Waterleaf at Catherine Creek in April.

Balsamroot
Balsamorhiza sagittata
Affirmation of the Wildflower: "I grow into my full potential"
Element: Fire, Earth

Aging • Confidence • Digestion • Depression • Ego • Empowerment • Fairy-Nature Realms • Father Issues • Grounding • Immunity • Inner-Fire • Leadership • Masculine/Men • Maturity • Mental Balance • Patience • Purpose • Responsibility • Self-esteem • Self-worth • Strength • Chakra 3 (solar plexus), 6 (3rd eye)

Balanced: mature masculine, or inner-masculine, presence that is patient, wise, warm, and grounded; a spiritual leader, elder, or Grandfather figure

An elder plant, Balsamroot grows ten years before the flowers bloom and live for 60-70 years. This radiant teacher plant shows you how to mature into your masculine (or inner-masculine) wisdom, patience, and deeply rooted leadership potential.

I call Balsamroot the *Sunflower of The Gorge*. It fills sunny hills with hundreds of large radiant yellow flowers. The wildflower takes an average of ten years to go from seed to flower. Over sixty more years it grows very deep roots and large vibrant solar flowers. I consider them wise and caring Grandfathers. I honor their age, maturity, and wisdom. This plant is an elder teacher.

Herbally, the resinous Balsamroot roots are used for colds and flu. I have made herbal cough medicine using the roots with other herbs. The very deep and long roots are resinous hence its name. They are included in respiratory and cough formulas to heal and build immunity. Balsamroot flower essence can be added to herbal medicine to expand its ability to reach into emotional and spiritual aspects of an illness.

Balsamroot is a plant to heal the wounded masculine soul in the way the lily heals the feminine. The flower essence assists those who lack a healthy father or father figure. It brings us the frequency we may be missing. As I was walking by a Balsamroot at Tom McCall Rowena Preserve in Oregon, I heard the word "Shiva." Shiva, to the Hindu, is the Lord of Creation and represents the masculine creative energy—dynamic expression and knowledge.

The flower essence helps us honor the process of growth and aging. It helps us grow up, mature, and step into spiritual leadership. If there are parts of us that feel arrested in development or too ego-involved, Balsamroot can help those parts grow up... and reach their full potential. It can help build self-confidence through 3rd chakra support of our power center. Balsamroot is patient; it holds a steady fire like the sun.

This flower teaches us to radiate warmth, strength, and confidence. It lifts depression and gifts us with the light of the sun in the dark of winter. Its solar energy balances our will. It can also teach men, women, and children to honor life passages. At any age, there is perfection in the timing of the natural growth and maturation process.

• Sara, a small child, kept telling her mother, "I don't want to grow up. I don't want to grow up." Her mother gave her Balsamroot flower essence. Shortly after, Sara stopped saying it; she accepted and embraced the possibilities of getting older.

• Julie felt an energy surge through her spine and a feeling of masculine energy when she took the essence. It gave her a sense of a comforting father taking care of her, and that everything is okay when he is nearby. She felt more balanced and could stand taller. Julie found herself attracted to other golden-yellow colored flowers during the time she took the essence.

• Aimee felt Balsamroot flower essence align her spine and open the energy in her hands and feet. She felt it strengthened her yoga practice and allowed her to be supportive and wise in how she assisted her yoga students. She felt more connected to the Earth, very present, good, confident, and strong. It also warmed her. She experienced a more observing nature and felt like it took her roots deeper than the Sunflower essence had.

- During a Balsamroot Fire Ceremony, Sommerfawn found many ways to describe her experience of the Balsamroot's energy including: collective will, solar oneness, aligning the personal will with the solar will, inner strength, protection of the power center, peace with the Sun. She found its affects strong in helping her build her inner-fire and digestion.

Balsamroot inspired her to receive a Sun-Song. She shared, "I love how the Balsamroot makes me feel OK about being a 'late bloomer' or 'slow developer' and a person who has never managed to bring my full power or potential forth. I have also felt like I was 'wilted' or 'stunted in growth.' I hope to BURST FULLY FORTH in this life!"

Meet Balsamroot at Tom McCall Preserve at Rowena in April or May.

Barrett's Penstemon
Penstemon barrettiae
Affirmation of the Wildflower: "*I know I can fly*"
Element: Air, Fire

Anxiety • Children • Delight • Empowerment • Fairy-Nature Realms • Fear • Freedom • Inner-child • Joy • Leap-of-Faith • Masculine/Men • Motivation • Movement • Responsibility • Rites of Passage • Surrender • Self-pity • Strength • Stress • Transition • Trust • Vision Quest • Chakra 1 (root)

Balanced: trusting in life's joy by surrendering to freedom

Are you standing on the edge of a cliff getting ready to take a *leap of faith*? Barrett's Penstemon will help you trust that you will land safely. Go ahead and take the leap. This wildflower grows high in the basalt cliffs of The Gorge and nowhere else on earth.

Barrett's Penstemon grows in bushy clumps on the cliffs of the Columbia River Gorge. Against the dark basalt rock, they are a stunningly beautiful pinkish purple color that joyfully enlightens the landscape. When I attuned with them I felt pure joy resonating from within and delight in the moment. Fairies fly playfully around me asking me to come along and play, too.

This flower empowers us to surrender to the resonance of joy. Take a leap of faith. Just do it. The word *penstemon* means five stamens (stamens are the *penises* of a plant). This masculine active energy is a force that helps us break free by releasing fear. The flower essence frees patterns of fear, feeling stuck, or containing too much energy, especially in the root chakra. Instead, we can allow it to flow. It enhances our ability to respond with courage and align with freedom. One woman called Barrett's Penstemon her *saving grace*.

Barrett's Penstemon helps motivate us and make the commitment to move forward and to follow through by taking action steps. I have used this flower essence with great success for those who are prepared to move forward but something still holds them back. Are you ready to fly but resist? A few drops of the essence are often all we need to let go and fly empowered and free!

"I am pure divine joy
fairies fluttering with delight
I am uniquely you, too
no one else is alike

In happiness and flight
I open you to mysteries
and discoveries of your Soul

Don't delay refreshment
of your time and place
if you want freedom
take a step
into space

Let me hold your wings
and teach you how to soar
up in the stratosphere
and so much more

Let's play now and
become full of light
freeing up spaces
for greater delight

We love to fly with you and
see you soar
There is nothing else
to do but
more"

• In a flower essence study group, we all took Barrett's Penstemon flower essence. Each person had a very personal and profound experience of the flower. The energy of the flower reached different places for each one of us, and it brought us all together in great joy as a community. One woman had a very deep re-connection with her true sense of Self. She was boldly told by the Deva of the flower: "Get on your path and follow your dreams and your joy, now!"

• Cynthia felt like she was perched on the edge of a cliff in fear of taking the next step. She knew in her mind that she would take it, but she still felt energetically and emotionally paralyzed. After taking Barrett's Penstemon she felt lighter and was able to step through her fear with ease.

• After working with her inner-child in a healing session, Maureen took a few drops of Barrett's Penstemon and experienced energy moving strongly into her root chakra. "I felt like the aura around my inner-child just lit up all around her. She's really happy! I am going to keep taking the essence for her." After a few days of using the essence she said. "The Barrett's Penstemon is fantastic. It's very nurturing."

Meet Barrett's Penstemon in the cliffs on the way to Catherine Creek in April.

Beacon Rock

Affirmation of Place: "I honor the sacred lands and walk with The Ancestors"

Balanced: a sense of belonging by walking with The Ancestors and spirits of land

Called *Che Che op tin*, navel of the world, Beacon Rock is a Native American gathering site. The spirits of the land welcome people to gather here, walk with them, and celebrate life. Walk with loving intention and you will feel a sense of belonging wherever you are.

"Beacon Rock Shares Its Light
We walked up Beacon Rock to join the walk of the Ancestors, the spirits of land, and nature elementals. We walked up Beacon Rock to honor the sacred lands that we now call home... and in that walk, the land became our home-lands. We now claim these lands as our home-lands, because we want to take care of them. We are the protectors of these lands."

As guest teacher for *Elderberry School of Botanical Medicine*, I took a group of students to Beacon Rock, a huge monolith of stone that towers above the Columbia River like a sentinel. I knew we would have a powerful experience. The spirits of the land had called us to this place.

We paused upon entered the forest. We gave an *offering*, and I asked the students to tune into the spirits of the land and see if they received any impressions. Someone offered, "this is an important gathering place and the land wants more people to come and gather here." Someone else sensed that a Deva was handcuffed. Another felt the suppression of the voices of the nature spirits. We held compassionate presence and loving intention for the openings that were needed during our walk and ceremony at the top. We felt the forest relax with our intentions, because we were present and listening from a place of love.

Different flowers and trees and elemental energies came into view as we climbed higher up the switchback trail on the pinnacle of stone. We walked with the intention of appreciation and gratitude. We walked with love for the plants and the beautiful lands and Columbia River in view below. It felt like we were walking with our own ancestors, the plants, and Ancestors of the land. As we walked higher on the 800 foot rock we rose higher in spirit. The wind in the firs sweetened the rarified air as we reached the summit. At the top, we made offerings, sang songs, visualized healing, and asked to connect and co-create with the elementals of earth, fire, water, air, and ethers. We had a beautiful time opening to the spirit of the rock, plants, elementals, and waters.

Afterwards, we talked about our experience as a profound gathering. Walking this walk with The Ancestors helped one woman claim these lands as her own. Now, she wanted to care for them and become a steward for the land and waters. Before today, she never felt like she truly belonged here. I saw this truth mirrored in the eyes, and nods, of the others. More importantly, I could sense it in their bodies. We had walked up Beacon Rock to honor the sacred lands that we now call home. We now claim these lands as our *home-lands*, because we want to take care of them. We held hands with The Ancestors in Oneness. We belong to these lands, too. We want to acknowledge, thank, and honor the indigenous people and their ancestors. We want to remember them and their *earthwalk*. We make amends to the people who came before, their descendants, and our Mother Earth.

Beacon Rock essence of place grounds us into the energy of the ancient Ancestors of the land through the navel of the world. Through our umbilicus, we connect back to our own mother and her mother and back through our lineage, we connect with the Grandmothers of Creation. It reminds us to find a place in nature where we want to belong. Take care of this place. Spend time there, gather with others, walk with sacred intention to connect with the nature spirits and ancestors and guardians of place. Be with the spirit of land and listen. Create a long-term relationship. Honor The Ancestors. Support the indigenous people. Make offerings. Give back. Make amends. The Ancestors' love is eternal.

Bleeding Heart
Dicentra formosa
Affirmation of the Wildflower: "*I cleanse my heart with love*"
Element: Air

Abandonment • Attachment • Betrayal • Breath • Co-dependence • Compassion • Forgiveness • Grief • Guilt • Heart Healing • Purification • Loss • Relationships • Resentment • Unconditional Love • Vulnerability • Chakra 4 (heart)

Balanced: open-hearted and healthy in loving relationships with self, others, and the past

You'll find the delicate heart-shaped flowers in the moist woods where the fairies hang out. This wildflower wants to remind you to create an open space for unconditional love in your heart. Breathe in love to fill it up often. That way it's easier to cope with the loss of loved ones, relationships, and old attachments.

Walking to one of the numerous waterfalls in The Gorge is the best place to see the brightly colored red hearts of the Bleeding Heart flowers. It appears that a drop of blood, or a tear, is flowing out of the flower. Someone must have designed this flower specifically for healing the heart. The flower is full of air like a balloon. The *Doctrine of Signatures* is clearly evident as the color and shape signifies its purpose of healing the heart, and it heals with a light, airy ease by giving our heart new space for love free of attachments.

The Bleeding Heart flower essence gives us the support needed to move through relationship changes, let go of emotional attachments that may include energetic cords, and move on even when we have lost a loved one to death, separation, or divorce. It honors and assists our grieving process by catalyzing tears and emotional release. When we allow ourselves to sit at the table with grief, it can break our heart open to greater love and joy.

Just a few drops of this flower essence may bring emotions to the surface so be gentle and seek assistance and emotional support if needed.

Bleeding Heart cleanses our heart chakra with compassion as it helps us release the past and move into the present. The essence gives us the capacity to let go of what we are holding onto so we can forgive. By releasing energetic cords or attachments to others, we free ourselves to love spaciously and unconditionally. By releasing fear of loss or abandonment, we become available for beautiful relationships again.

• Joanne boldly stood up during a class I taught to share her experience using the Bleeding Heart flower essence. She told us that she was very attached to her anger, resentment, and the hurt in her heart regarding a former boyfriend. She was very resistant to trying the Bleeding Heart flower essence. She called me several times over a few months period before finally ordering the essence. When she took Bleeding Heart it changed her life! She told us she tried to hold onto her old feelings, hurt, and pain, but she said she just couldn't. They were gone. It felt miraculous to her. She forgave her old boyfriend, and others, and healed herself. She was very grateful to move on.

Meet Bleeding Heart in moist woods like Eagle Creek Trail in May.

Buttercup
Ranunculus species
Affirmation of the Wildflower: "It's time to play!"
Element: Fire

Abuse • Ancestor Healing • Children • Confidence • Depression • Embodiment • Empowerment • Fairy-Nature Realms • Forgiveness • Happiness • Inner-child • Innocence • Play • Pain • Relationships • Self-doubt • Self-pity • Self-worth • Shame • Transformation • Trauma • Trust • Chakra 1 (root), 3 (solar plexus), 6 (3rd eye)

Balanced: ability to play and experience the sweet innocence and wonder of a magical child

Buttercup petals are lustrous like sunshine. The fairies of Buttercup delight in expanding your ability to play and experience the sweet innocence and wonder of a precious, magical child. This wildflower expands your self-worth and capacity for fun.

The Buttercup fairies were trying to attract my attention. "We want to play. Come make an essence with us!" I walked through their carpet of bright yellow wildflowers as they vibrantly danced with the sun and vivid blue sky. I laid the bowl of water in the thick stand of Buttercups and instantly a number of blossoms leapt into the water. It's always a treat to meet enthusiastic flower fairies when creating a flower essence.

Shiny, sweet yellow Buttercups are childhood favorites for many. Buttercups are the flower we put under our chin to see if yellow appears reflected on our skin. If it does, we like butter! These flowers are especially suited for embracing the innocence and wonder of the child and our inner-child. It re-connects us with the fairy realms and our true self-worth.

The first time I created a flower essence with them, I heard the fairies sing, "You are my sunshine, my only sunshine, you make me happy when skies are gray, you never know dear how much I love you, please don't take my sunshine away." Songs are a common way for flowers to communicate. They like to sing songs that we know or make up songs or tones. They want us to listen really carefully and see if we hear their music… or their beautiful tones. The fairies want to connect with us.

When we look deep into our own inner essence, we find the *child of awareness*. She or he is at our inner core. If our child feels cared for and happy, s/he is full of wonder, delight, and joy. If not, Buttercup helps bring this child back to us. The flower essence can help open us to creating a stronger bond with our inner-child (or own children) by listening, being present, and accepting the feelings of the past. The Buttercup fairies heal us through childhood songs and ties to the fairy kingdom. Taking the flower essence asks our sense of worthiness, wonder, and happiness to return. But we must be willing to play more and take good care of our inner-child.

When I have used Buttercup flower essence, it seems to solidify and strengthen my 3rd chakra and personal will. It helps me take action on behalf of my inner-child's needs. Many of us didn't develop a healthy will as children—knowing what we truly want and need and desire and how to ask for it. Buttercup is a sunny alternative that reaches the core of our self-worth. It helps us feel more comfortable to be fully present in our body. Sometimes childhood trauma keeps us from staying fully grounded in our bodies. Buttercup helps us find joy and delight in our physical self.

"Twinkling and flying and sparkling with light
The fairies of Buttercup spark my delight
Many gather to giggle and play
And when it's time they all go away

But when I come near
They are kind, generous, and oh so curious
They engage in rhythms and dances and
find ways to be mostly glorious

They make me feel like I am a magical child
like I was born wild"

- Dani used Buttercup flower essence to bring clarity and compassion to the memories of the past. As new memories surfaced around past relationships and childhood sexual abuse, she would take the essence several times a day. She noticed that the memories would come but not overwhelm her. The essence encouraged her to ask how she could nurture herself versus feeling fear or dread. The Buttercup Fairies would shine their joy and brightness into the spaces that had been cleared and released.

- Katie S. wrote: "I love the sassy yellow buttercup blossoms that pop up all over Prairie Star Meadows. The plant is very hardy, pervasive, strong and insistent. I experience Buttercup flower essence as an activation of my will forces in the lower half of my body. It invokes a feeling of confidence, initiation, grounded power, action, focus and determination. The song I heard when I first took the Buttercup essence was:

> *"Everything's Okay! A Okay!*
> *Today is your day! It's A Okay!*
> *The way has been made! It's A okay!*
> *Align your will with the divine play!*
> *Be all that you are today!"*

A little dance came with it of rooting down into my hips, solar plexus and feet with strength, sass and confidence."

"I take this essence when I need to accomplish tasks or move ahead with a project or a new way of being. It helps me to believe in myself and my ability to accomplish tasks and be my true self in the world. Buttercup essence has been helpful with clients who experience inertia or resistance to taking healthy action. It is a support in overcoming obstacles, taking action and courageously stepping out in the world to strut their stuff and offer their authentic gifts!"

- To Abby, "Buttercup feels like a little munchkin full of energy, confidence and charisma. So chippery with a go-get-em kind of attitude. It's so optimistic, ambitious and positive! It has been a very light-hearted, supportive, motivating energy in my life. I would highly recommend it if you are feeling a lack of motivation, depression, or self-doubt."

Meet Buttercup on The Dalles Mountain Road in March.

California Poppy

Eschscholzia californica
Affirmation of the Wildflower: "I love myself; I value myself"
Element: Earth, Fire, Water, Air, Ethers

Appreciation • Balance • Beauty • Children • Clairvoyance • Creativity • Emotional Cleansing • Fairy-Nature Realms • Grounding • Hormone Balance • Illness • Individuality • Integration • Intuition • Meridian Cleanser • Projection • Psychic Development • Receptivity • Relationship • Rites of Passage • Self image • Self-worth • Shadow • Chakras 3 (sacral), 4 (heart), 5 (throat), 6 (3rd eye)

Balanced: owning and treasuring our inner-beauty and preciousness

The vibrant, shiny orange flower spirits help you claim, own, and treasure your own inner-beauty, light, and gifts. There is no need to project your magnificence onto others. Appreciate yourself more and your self-value will grow. You are precious.

The most striking thing about California Poppy is its bright orange color and beautiful sheen that graces its delicate petals. Its color is very attractive to the eyes, and the Soul, and it brightens up any dull feelings with its magical presence. Children love this flower. It likes to dazzle in the rays of the sun and fill up its shiny cup with sunlight. Its petals close up for the night.

California Poppy as a flower essence has many uses. It can be taken when we want to feel more appreciated and valued. When something appreciates, like a house, it builds value. This essence helps us truly appreciate and treasure ourselves, and feel self-love. The flower mirrors awareness of the beauty that surrounds us and therefore is within us and our own heart. Instead of focusing on or projecting onto the great beauty we see in others, we can claim our own inner-beauty as a reflection.

The essence can help us open to source energy and awaken our psychic gifts in a balanced way. This includes our relationship and connection with the fairy and spiritual realms. California Poppy can help us integrate and re-align during times of spiritual expansion or physic opening. Gurudas in *Flower Essences and Vibrational Medicine*, says California Poppy was created "to augment the body's evolution by cleansing the meridians." And, "A need for psychic and spiritual balance is a major indicator for prescribing this essence. Universal essence for "expediting emotional cleansing." It also opens artist's creativity.

After a meditation with the flower Deva, fairies circled over me in beautiful colors of joy. I felt their petals' shimmering light sparkling through my energy field...

> *"California Poppy reminds people to view themselves and be seen in the light of God"*
> *"My heart is bursting with a presence of me!"*
> *"Nourishes your being with light"*
> *"Beauty grows from the heart"*

I have used California Poppy flower essence to cleanse ley lines on the Earth—Earth meridians—by placing drops of the flower essence on the land and in waterways with love and gratitude. During a land clearing ceremony, I placed several drops of California Poppy and Glacier Lily flower essences into the river. To our amazement, a flock of geese flying above us immediately turned around and flew back over our heads to come closer and land in the river nearby. My client's reply: *"I've never seen that before."* I responded, *"Neither have I."*

- This flower helped Chris V. move out of the feeling of not being appreciated enough in her relationship. She felt better as she moved into stronger gratitude and acceptance of herself and the positive gifts her boyfriend offered.

- Cynthia needed California Poppy. She was having trouble seeing her own self and her patterns during interaction with her birth family. The essence helped her clear her own projections onto her siblings, and gave clarity about her siblings' projections onto her, so she could bring her focus back to valuing and loving herself, first.

Camilla Blossom Bishop
Nature Spirit Alchemy

MENU

Workshops: Land Connecting Protocols
Learn how to create harmonious relationship with land through empowering teachings and protocols. Connect with the spirit of land—the unseen realms, elementals, fairies, unicorns, ancestors, flower devas, sacred waters. Create altars and magical gardens. Big Island, Hawaii & USA Tour 2018 (Seeking land hosts.)

Custom Flower Essence Formula
with *Sacred Spirit Deck* Intuitive Card Reading
Receive subtle energy medicine from sacred flowers to nurture and support emotional healing, creativity, and spiritual blossoming.
$65/45 minutes & formula (add $7 shipping) phone or in-person

Healing Session
Feel supported in rebirthing and/or aligning with your true nature. Nature spirit alchemy, subtle energy healing, ancestor lineage healing, fairy shamanism, and/or land connecting protocols.
$80/hour phone +$25/with flower essence formula ($7 shipping)

Mentorship
Land Connecting Protocols
Flower Essence Alchemy

ETSY Shop
Flower Essences, Formulas, Books, Cards, Kits, and more.
ETSY Shop link: CamillaBlossom.com

CamillaBlossom.com camillablossom1111@gmail.com

- Monica offers her students the essence of California Poppy to take and to rub in their palms before she teaches Qi Gong classes.

Meet California Poppy along most roadsides of The Gorge in May.

Camas

Camassia quamash
Affirmation of the Wildflower: "I am open to everything, attached to nothing."
Element: Water

Acceptance • Ancestor Healing • Attachment • Balance • Brain Hemisphere Balance • Ceremonial • Communication • Depression • Duality • Immunity • Integration • Focus • Grief • Grounding • Mental Balance • Sound Healing • Spiritual Communication • Spiritual Guidance • Trust • Chakra 6 (3rd eye)

Balanced: reverence and balance in a pure state of acceptance of what is

In making a flower essence of Camas, I had a vision of a large Native American chief spreading his arms wide to form a rainbow and speaking the affirmation above. Camas blossoms mirror the quality of pure acceptance and appear like a serene sea of blue. The bulbs of the sacred Camas are gathered and eaten at Native American ceremonial feasts.

Camas's serene blue color blankets whole meadows in the spring like a sea of water. The wildflower is a sacred plant to the native tribes of the Northwest. When I made the flower essence I felt a complete circle of Native American ancestral spirits surrounding me. I could tell this plant was very sacred to the indigenous people of these lands.

The flower essence of Camas provides a model of energy mastery by balancing polarized energies, for example thinking and feeling. It assists in balancing the two hemispheres of the brain. By opening and easing emotional flow, Camas activates under-active parts of our brain and the corpus callosum that connects right-brain and left-brain. A balanced brain makes for a balanced human because of the full integration of intuitive/rational, being/doing, and feminine/masculine aspects. This wildflower is in the feminine lily family yet brings a gender-fluid presence. Men attending my wildflower walk were very drawn to this wildflower.

Camas helps us get in the right frame of mind. It helps us build more trust in our knowing and objectivity for a calmer, more unified presence. I've had a number of Camas experiences that have reminded me of my power to seamlessly *know*. Our knowing strengthens when we are in a state of accepting what is. There is no need for attachment.

Carlin, a dear friend and employee of my flower essence business, was on her deathbed with cancer. Carlin was very connected with nature. She loved the wildflowers and the flower essences I created. Nance and I planted 100 Camas bulbs in Carlin's honor at a wetland in Washington. We held the bulbs in our hands and prayed for Carlin and invited in the Deva of the Camas flowers. We blessed each bulb we planted with a drop of the Camas flower essence. Halfway through the planting we paused. Huge waves of energy that felt like Carlin's presence moved through the landscape. The hairs on our skin prickled. As Nance and I drove home these words came through… *pure acceptance*. Carlin passed over three days later. Planting the Camas was a healing balm for loss, and it will be a joyous gift to see the wildflowers' serene blue blooms blanket the wetland area each spring.

Recently we planted Camas bulbs on the land where I live. As we planted, tears of gratitude ran down our cheeks. I could feel and see The Ancestors stir with joy that the wild Camas would return to the area. It was very moving. A spirit guardian came forward and gifted me with something because he was so grateful. He wanted to join us in creating a land sanctuary. Camas has shown up when I am communing across the veils or something's life force is nearing death. It is an awakener.

• Dan first encountered Camas during one of my workshops. He recalled that the first flower we encountered was a white lily and the women in the class were particularly drawn to it. Camas was the second flower we encountered and the men in the class had a special connection with it. It was really the first time that Dan felt a special connection to a flower. Since then, Camas resonates with him. He makes sure that he always has some on hand, and usually takes it along with whatever other essence he is taking. The Camas affirmation—*open to everything, attached to nothing*—has become "a mantra for me, and a key to my spiritual growth," said Dan.

- Witnessing the state of the world, Ellie accessed her broken-hearted place within as she tried to forgive humanity… including herself. She was guided to use Camas to let go of her attachments. Shortly after taking the flower essences she had a chance to practice. A highly anticipated employee she hired during a three month long hiring process suddenly backed out. She didn't know why but felt there was a higher purpose for this development. Ellie found Camas essence to be "really beneficial. If I ask, it's showing me what I need to see and opening up windows and doors that were shut. I shut down for self-preservation and to defend myself. I'm practicing detachment. Things have been hidden away for a reason. I feel gratefully humble and in a state of appreciation. I can see and feel in a good way. It's easier to forgive myself."

Meet Camas at Catherine Creek in April.

Catherine Creek Arch
Affirmation of Place: "I am a bridge to the cosmos"

Balanced: activated *spirit fire* and connection to celestial energy of the sun, the moon, and the stars

This huge natural stone arch is also a bridge. Set against a basalt backdrop, this sacred site acts as a multidimensional portal connecting cosmic and earth consciousness. It opens a doorway to the Star Nations and transformative shamanic journeys. Respect the power of this place. It can help you remember your true origins.

The trails at Catherine Creek are a beautiful place to see among 90 varieties of amazing wildflowers in the spring, sit with ancient teacher trees like Ponderosa Pines, Oak, and a colony of Bigleaf Maples, view the scenic river, and sing with a sweet creek in the heat of the sun. Many of the wildflowers in this book grow here as well as the rarer Dutchman's Breeches and the exquisite Bitterroot. At one point on the trail, there is a round etheric doorway where I always stop and give an offering and ask permission to enter from the guardian spirit of the land. This way, I enter the higher dimensions of the sacred site with the support and blessing of the protector spirits. It is a very different experience. I always receive very special experiences and profound healing by honoring the invisible realms.

I am often called to visit Catherine Creek and its massive arch during times of transition. I have noticed how it calls to those that want to open their relationship with the energies of The Gorge, the celestial energies, and to those who are ready for their next level of spiritual initiation.

The Arch at Catherine Creek is a holy place of great mystery. Every time I approach the arch I feel I am approaching ancient wise ones that bridge planet earth to the cosmos. I feel very small and humbled and very expansive and multidimensional at the same time. It is very sacred to the indigenous people. It serves as a *portal* to journey back to celestial bodies—the sun, the moon, and the stars—to activate our Spirit so our *spirit fire* can burn brighter.

Across the Columbia River in Mosier, Oregon I hiked to the viewpoint above Mosier Creek. I glanced across to Washington state at the Catherine Creek area and was stunned to see the arch rising up like a magical site on the horizon. In all my years exploring the area, I never knew this view. Somehow it registered in an interesting way almost like a shock. I realized that Catherine Creek Arch is overlooking the lands in a much more prominent and powerful way than I had expected. It is casting its energy far and wide.

Catherine Creek Arch essence of place offers a bridge to our multidimensional celestial self so we can activate our *spirit fire*—the flame of our eternal spiritual light. Experience the sun, the moon, and the stars through this portal. We can connect here with aspects of our cosmic self and an expanded view of who we are and where we come from. For those bigger questions in life, this arch moves us towards even greater mysteries.

Desert Sage
Artemisia tridentata
Affirmation of the Wildflower: "I hold sacred space"
Element: Earth, Fire, Water, Air, Ethers

Ancestor Healing • Boundaries • Ceremonial • Channeling • Clarity • Clearing • Earth Mother • Embodiment • Connection • Inner-Shaman • Mental Balance • Purification • Protection • Sacred Space • Self-respect • Chakras 4 (heart), 5 (throat), 6 (3rd eye)

Balanced: feel protected, clear minded, and honoring of the sacred space of our body; inner-shaman

Desert Sage, or Sagebrush, is gathered and dried in a sacred manner and used in medicine pouches and bundles, ceremony, and burned as smudge before ceremony to cleanse the energy of space, people, and to honor the holy ones. The plant's powerful cleansing and protective medicine can be experienced when you crush the highly aromatic leaves and smell them. Create sacred space for yourself with the spirit of Desert Sage.

The plant's spirit gathers elemental energies of fire, water, air, and earth to create a fragrant, thick, and strong energy field that is potent and protective and covers the hillsides and desert landscape where it grows. The hills near the banks of the Deschutes River are covered in Desert Sage. Its fragrance is so potent it feels like we are entering another dimensional space—too much inhalation of the potent leaves may even cause nausea. Its spirit holds us is its pure power—like a cloud of light energy. Ancestors are present where this plant grows. As an *Artemisia*, it is considered sacred to the Lunar Goddess, Artemis.

Desert Sage is the native sacred purification plant, and it creates a protective container of sacred space. Creating sacred space is such an important way to maintain our positive energy, hold what is ours, release what is not, stay in connection with all there is, and keep ourselves clear. I burn our local Desert Sage as a grounding and clearing smudge before ritual, ceremony, or to clear my energy or space. Smoke that rises from burning dried leaves can envelope space, bodies, and objects to bless them with clearing waves of this earth plant. We honor the spirit realms and ancestors when we show up clean. I love using our regional plant medicine because it carries a strong spirit of place and connects us to fire and the river and The Ancestors who have used this plant through the generations.

We are sacred. Our body is sacred. Desert Sage honors and protects and reminds us to hold this knowing. In one visionary experience, I saw a Desert Sage male spirit adorning me with the plant's silvery-gray leaves. I had become a sacred holy woman—White Buffalo Calf Woman. He was honoring me as the Goddess as I felt waves of pure light moving inside my body clearing away energy and lower vibrations. I heard vibrational tones rise, within my auditory awareness, to a higher pitch and a new melody. I was with the sacred ancestors in peace and stillness. The spirit made waves with his hands and sent ecstatic bliss coursing through my sacred body.

Our body is a temple—a sacred container for our soul to make deeper connection with Mother Earth and Source Creator. This medicine puts us in touch with the holiness of our body. Desert Sage flower essence replenishes our inner-nature so our body can be experienced as sacred space. Clearing and honoring our body garners self-respect and mirrors our relationship with the Mother Earth. Appropriate boundaries can be created.

As *water medicine*, or a flower essence, Desert Sage can be taken as drops added to water to clear our energy from within. It purifies our sacredness by sweeping or washing away old energy. It shows up when we need to clear old energy including beliefs, thoughts, negativity, or mental attitudes. The essence can help us create a stronger field of energy by focusing on our thought process and how that affects our auric boundaries. Positive thoughts strengthen our energy system. Clearing our energy renews and clears our mind, body, and spirit. It shows us how to embrace our sacred Self and inner-shaman.

The flower essence is a great tool that is indicated when we feel disconnected, blocked or bothered by external energies, or are experiencing negative thinking, monkey-mind, or anxiety. It can be very helpful for empaths or sensitive souls to cleanse their energy fields. Take internally or use the flower essence as a *water smudge* by adding a few drops to a water spray atomizer bottle and spray around the aura—the body's energy field—or space. Let water purify the energy or use a feather to circulate it further. Desert Sage flower essence was a key ingredient in a sacred space aromatherapy-flower essence clearing spray I used to make and market widely.

• Katie S. wrote, "Desert Sage channeled essence has a very high spiritual vibration. It is facilitating my connection with the angels and with spiritual truth and clarity."

When attending a shamanic breathwork training, Katie used the flower essence to clear their energy field when smudge with Desert Sage smoke was not available, and it worked very effectively.

• Hannah was feeling off and had been experiencing two days of anxiety when she took the flower essence. She could feel the energy of the desert and of snakes and a sense of being dried out. A sense of calm overtook her.

• Inez heard the words: *Protector of Sacred* when she used the flower essence. It showed her how to open her crown chakra more and to access deeper grounding by staying in her body and calling spiritual energy down and into her body. The plant spirits purified her by dunking her in water. Then, she was placed in fire. She felt her body get hot, she yawned, felt a bit of nausea, and felt her solar plexus clear. "The plant medicine was going to the places where I had impurities and was burning it up. It told me that I am sacred and that I need to demonstrate my sacredness in the way I walk in the world. This will benefit everyone."

• Laura J. was very fidgety and unsettled in her seat and her mind had been busy lately. On taking some Desert Sage, she immediately felt her body sink into stillness. She didn't want to move. She felt like a porous stone being comforted and held. She felt at peace. Her mind was calm.

• Abby had a shamanic experience when she took the flower essence of

Desert Sage. A rattlesnake ate her head and its fangs rested on her neck sucking out water (her emotions) and drying her out. A wall crumbled and as pieces of her fell they became Sage and burned up. A *cord releasing* healing process that she had worked with during the previous week came in, and she saw the plant spirit apply black salve-like burnt medicine on the places where the energetic cords needed to be released and healed. Desert Sage told her it will "make the decision for her about which cords need to go." Abby experienced the medicine as powerful and sweet. She described its actions as a gentle cleanup after healing. Two words came to her: *Flush Residue*. (Releasing energetic cords frees up our life-force energy by clearing unhealthy or old attachments, relationships, healing processes, emotional-mental energy, belief patterns, and karma.)

Meet Desert Sage along the mouth of the Deschutes River, Oregon.

Fairy Slipper Orchid
Calypso bulbosa
Affirmation of the Wildflower: "I open to new adventures"
Element: Earth, Water

Abundance • Ancestor Healing • Ascension • Assertiveness • Teleportation • Change • Culture Shock • Fairy-Nature Realms • Fear • Fertility • Illusion • Intimacy • Jet-lag • Masculine/Feminine Balance • Pleasure • Safety • Sensitivity • Sexuality • Touch • Travel • Truth • Chakra 2 (sacral), 4 (heart), 6 (3rd eye), 7 (crown)

Balanced: willing to enter new places, new realms, and experience new ways of being

New paths and travels await you. Slip on a pair of fairy slippers and enter the hidden realms of Fairyland for a joyful excursion into your creative imagination. The spirit of the wildflower will help you go to new places… and find your way if you get lost.

This orchid is a mysterious beauty that grows in sheltered forests of Oregon and Washington. Very sensual, beautiful, delicate and elusive— *Calypso* is a word that signifies *concealment*. Its petals fan out to create wings on its slippers. Pink, purples, reds of the pouch-like slipper create intricate patterns of spotted colors. Around a white lip appears a fuzzy yellow beard. Its appearance may vary. Newly emerging queen bumblebees are attracted to the wildflower's bright colors yet no nectar awaits so they do not return. Some call the wildflower Angel Slipper, Venus Slipper, or Deer-head Orchid due to its silhouette.

Fairy Slipper Orchids only make itself known to those it wishes to relate with. This orchid may seem delicate, but it knows exactly what it wants. I've been on forest walks with crowds of self-focused people that walk by colonies of these pink beauties. The fairies want it that way. They do not mess around. Often, photos come out blurry. They have communicated they don't want to be touched by most people. They do not like to be disturbed nor do they transplant well. Remember to ask permission if you want to go near them or take a photograph.

Many of the qualities of the Fairy Slipper: spending time in the shade of others, being concealed, fearful of change or new places or disturbance are indications for using the flower essence. Flowers mirror our nature, current state, or situation. The wildflower love their true nature and can teach us how to love these aspects of ourselves, too. And, it can teach us how to open to change and embrace new ways of being. Orchids are great for daring us to transform our lives.

The first time I made this flower essence, I was with a friend, Riki, on her beautiful land in Washington near Panther Creek Falls. I cut a flower to use and instantly regretted it. The spirit of Fairy Slipper was teaching me how to slow down and listen more carefully. The flower showed me how to place the bowl underneath its stem and the flower spirit would beam glorious pink and purple frequencies of its light frequencies into the water to create the flower essence. It was not necessary to pick the wildflower for the medicine. Fairy Slipper holds a very subtle high frequency and prefers to heal on that subtle energetic level.

After making the flower essence it took some time to open to the flower once again. I kept asking, but still felt guilty about how I hastily picked the flower. When the spirit of Fairy Slipper chose to show up again it was in a dream about six months later. I sprang up in bed with these words: *I'm for fear of traveling to new places*. I was thrilled to receive this clear message and began taking it to help me with my own fears. I realized that new places could include physical locations as well as fairy realms, different dimensions, shamanic journeys, spiritual expansion and ascension, and forms of alternate reality which are unfamiliar. The orchid's masculine Venusian energy can help us use our hearts to direct our action.

• Darlene (not her real name) loved worked with Fairy Slipper flower essence as she traveled overseas in India and Nepal. Out of the blue, she called me to tell me she got the message from the Fairy Slipper Orchid that it was helping her with all forms of travel issues like jet-lag, culture shock, and general travel fears. This fit with the travel theme that Riki received: the essence could open our advanced abilities for teleportation, a way of transportation without using physical means.

• During a weekend flower essence workshop I was teaching, we were fortunate to have blooming Fairy Slipper Orchids in the forest. The spirit of the plant told me to focus on ancestor healing. We circled around the Fairy Slippers and one-by-one we took a few drops of a flower essence formula that we created for ourselves and our ancestors. We supported each person at she took her essence relaying any visions or impressions we received. As Ramona took her essence, she appeared to slip her feet into the fairy slippers and journey to connect with her ancestors and the fairy realms. A new awareness seemed to take hold of her and inform her relations with the land her family had been care-taking for many generations. After that, she never felt the same about Fairy Slipper Orchid. They transported her to a new consciousness and sense of connection to the spirit realms.

Meet Fairy Slipper Orchid on BZ Corners Rafting Trail (White Salmon River) in May.

Foxglove
Digitalis purpurea
Affirmation of the Wildflower: "Emotional vulnerability is a gift"
Element: Earth, Fire

Emotional Balance • Emotional Honesty • Fairy-Nature Realms • Fear • Grief • Heart Healing • Intimacy • Purification • Relationships • Self-love • Truth • Unconditional Love • Vulnerability • Chakra 4 (heart)

Balanced: ability to be intimate, vulnerable, and honest in relationship with self and others

Pure white or pale purple fairy hats line Foxglove's stalk. Foxglove opens new chambers of the heart and can activate emotional honesty. This plant is used for medical heart patients to re-start their hearts. Does your heart need a jolt from the Foxglove fairies to wake you up right now to a greater capacity for emotional expression?

Digitalis purpurea, Foxglove's scientific name, means *finger-like* because the blossoms fit nicely over our fingertips. Some belief its name came out of *folk's glove,* instead of the word *fox. Folk's glove* means *fairy folk.* Foxgloves are considered poisonous if ingested or the water from a vase of flowers is drunk. The medicine is used to control the heart-rate of heart patients. A no-pick or channeled flower essences is the safest way to ingest the healing qualities of this flower. If you are very sensitive, be gentle and make space to work with this flower essence as it can offer powerful healing experiences.

I was delighted to see eight-foot tall Foxgloves take over my medicine wheel garden with their delightful white and purple tubular-shaped spotted flowers. Fairies live inside the roomy blossoms and they streamed out of the mouth to travel around the garden. My medicine wheel garden was such a profound teacher. The fairies told me where to place it. "Make a circle," they sang. The garden and its flowers helped me create a new relationship with myself by being in relationship with them. I needed to renew my foundation after divorce and rediscover my own nature. I was so grateful; the perfect medicine always seems to arrive on my doorstep. As if by magic, the plants step forward when I need them. Foxglove grew tall for me… helping my heart open to healing.

I tend to be a private person. After divorcing in 2001, I became a single mother half-time and all my relationships shifted. It was a very vulnerable time, and I was not always skilled in sharing my true feelings, nor able to say what I wanted or needed. The Deva of Foxglove saw right through me and gave me a strong sense of self-acceptance even when I was less attuned to accepting myself. Later, I realized that making flower essences was for me, first. The flowers wanted me to love myself as much as they loved me. Foxglove was kin on my journey of self-love. I had a lot to learn about emotional self-honesty. What I learned strengthened my emotional exchanges in all my relationships.

The flower essence of Foxglove calms fears in the heart, fosters healthy vulnerability, and builds greater self-love. Its strong stalk reminds us to stand tall in our own truth and beauty. Foxglove wants us to find our truth by being willing to be honest with ourselves. The essence helps us move past our fear of exposure to welcome openings to greater intimacy and healing. Remember, the fairies will assist all who ask with a pure intention.

After taking some Foxglove essence, a troupe of Foxglove fairies gathered around my heart and patted it lightly with healing comfort to soothe my inner-child. She was pouting and sad and the Foxglove fairies helped invoke my adult presence to show her everything was okay with my heart. I felt prickly energy as the old fell away with the support of the fairy troupe of healers. They appeared like *scrubber fairies* cleaning and brightening me up. Then, the cup shape of the Foxglove flower flipped down to make a yoni shaped opening that revealed the way my heart healing was connected with my sexuality. The fairies offered healing to my womb area too. I had to take it easy as it opened a powerful healing process that continued throughout the day.

• Blue experiences Foxglove, her favorite flower, as a place to see fairies… if you were going to see them. She said it grows well in her garden and the colors are for the heart. "The fairies make hats with the flowers and urge us to come inside. Go inside to the depths. They seem to call you into a higher heart experience. They are not *out-there* flowers but ask us to *come inside* or *go within*."

• Laura found Foxglove activated her intuition. All these ideas flooded her mind. She felt she was tapping into a higher version of herself. "I feel abundant. I am going deep within—all the answers are already there!"

• When she took the flower essence, Abby's had an energetic and emotional purging experience. She is very sensitive to flower essences and felt it was important to set aside a designated space to purge when taking this flower essence. It is powerful in its affects to help let go of emotions and what is held inside. For her, it involved her throat. She also saw black birds fly out of her mouth (a Native American sign of energy clearing after ceremony).

• Inez shared, "At first I felt the Foxglove flower essence in my heart, and my heart had wings. My lung channel lit up. It was almost painful. White light was going through the channel. Very distinctive experience. The spirits of the plant worked on my lung channel and they worked on my throat, moving energy. Then a strong pressure—a big strong masculine being said: 'All right, let's go. I'm going to tell you more.' The energy was gentle and soft. 'We're going to water.' The water washed over me… neck down washing with sparkling pink water. 'Wash you off and remind you of your shine so you can see your own light.'"

Meet Foxglove in Larch Mountain Corridor in July.

Green Bog Orchid
Platanthera aquilonis
Affirmation of the Wildflower: "I align with the heart of Mother Earth"
Element: Earth

Ancestor Healing • Communication • Creativity • Death/Dying • Earth Mother Connection • Fairy-Nature Realms • Food Issues • Heart Healing • Immunity • Integration • Harmony • Hormone Balance • Intimacy • Masculine/Men • Mental Balance • Nourishment • Protection • Purpose • Receptivity • Relationships • Responsibility • Rites of Passage • Safety • Self-assertiveness • Self-pity • Sensitivity • Stress • Transformation • Womb Healing • Chakras 1 (root), 4 (heart), 5 (throat), 6 (3rd eye)

Balanced: grounded heartbeat connected to Earth Mother's heartbeat and the nature spirits

This potent green wild orchid expands your capacity to feel love and receive the constant supply of nourishment from the earth. Green flowers are precious finds in nature as they harmonize the heart, awaken communication with the nature spirits, and inspire creativity. Green Bog Orchid grounds your heart into Mother Earth's heart.

I'm always very excited to see the petite green flowers on Green Bog Orchid's slender stalk. Green flowers are nature connectors and inspire growth, prosperity, and intuitive awareness. I believe orchids are evolutionary catalysts that help us move from fear to love. In 2009, this flower spoke up powerfully. The orchid called itself a *Green Giant* and told me to…"Flood the world with this essence. The earth needs it now." The plant wants us to synchronize our heartbeat with the heartbeat of Mother Earth to make our hearts stronger.

The spirit of the Green Bog Orchid helps us receive the constant supply of nourishing earth energy from Mother Earth and all her green allies. Along with life-force energy, earth energy is necessary for vibrant health and happiness. It is healing yin energy. Earth energy circulates in our bodies and grounds out and cleanses our entire subtle energy system. Most dis-ease occurs because of lack of grounding and connection with earth energy.

Green Bog Orchid flower essence addresses our longing for heart connection and relationship; it can help us deeply connect to others by gratifying and harmonizing the heart. It opens our sensuality and frees repressive tendencies. I gave the essence to a group of women. Tears flowed as every single one felt her heart *and* womb energy ground deeply into the earth. The essence assists and activates our ability to attune with the nature spirits. Relationship can be expanded to embrace fairy and nature realms.

This flower essence was created on Mt. Hood in a boggy alpine meadow. The energy of the mountain is infused in the essence. I place drops of Green Bog Orchid in waterways and on Mother Earth to assist her shifting, and take drops in my water to assist with my own shifts. The Earth's *body* is like ours in that she heals through vibrational shifts. Flower essences are perfect medicine for her as well. Dropping essences on the land helps her clear human emotional debris and stagnation. Taking the essence, the frequencies circulate through our own energy field and to the earth.

In the Cedar forest, I gathered with a circle of women and we each took a few drops of the Green Bog Orchid flower essence. As soon as we took it, we felt a very strong energy movement coming from our collective heart space as it moved quickly and deeply into the heart of Mother Earth to ground us there. It was quite a powerful sensation. We all felt more present, aware, and connected to love, each other, and the Mother.

• Abby wrote, "When I started using Green Bog Orchid it told me to use it in the spring time and play in the forest with all of the nature spirits in their most abundant state. Being right in the heart of winter and that not being possible at the moment it urged me to mix every single flower essence that I have and bombard and immerse myself with the spirit of them all!"

• "Green Bog Orchid helps me connect with the green magic and helping spirits of the forest. I also use it very regularly with clients in my shamanic practice to assist people in healing through connecting with nature. I see that it helps people rekindle their innate connection with the healing green energy of the plants and life forces of nature," Katie S. wrote.

Meet Green Bog Orchid in Mt. Hood Meadow in July.

Heart-leaf Buckwheat
Eriogonum compositum var. compositum
Affirmation of the Wildflower: "*I am comfortable with change*"
Element: Earth

Change • Control Issues • Comfort Food (light body) • Detoxification • Exhaustion • Fear • Food Issues • Grounding • Illness • Immunity • Mental Balance • Nourishment • Resistance • Stability • Transition • Worry • Chakra 3 (solar plexus), 4 (heart), 7 (crown)

Balanced: comfortable in embracing change

The colorful flower Deva of the Heart-leaf Buckwheat whispered to me: "*We are comfort food for the light body.*" They remind you that it is best to relax, feel comforted, and go with the change, transition, and new life. Ask them to assist you when you feel out of control.

The native wildflowers Heartleaf Buckwheat are hardy, easy to grow, and create a field of light wherever they live. The flowers are soft creamy-colored and very hardy, but the Heart-leaf Buckwheat Deva is pastel shades of yellow, green, and purple. The heavenly flower looks like a soft cloudy pillow that we want to lay down on and sleep. Change, change, and more change can make us feel sleepy.

I eat comfort food when going through change, and I was inspired by the idea of *energetic* comfort food for our aura (light body). This wildflower feeds our nervous system and aura with nourishing light as it grounds out stress. It brightens up our being and comforts us when we feel out of control or are in a state of worry. Some experience this as a courage-building process. It also loosens up tightness in the body and helps releasing of energies of the past.

Heart-leaf Buckwheat eases change, resistance, and inertia. It can also comfort us when memories of change surface. It helps us move out of ruts, routines, and old behaviors. It also brings comfort and nourishment to the core of our being and helps us support and sustain ourselves through change. We learn to dance with light and change and energy as is, in the moment.

> *"Stability and certainty*
> *is what you think you want*
> *But change is all around*
> *and it is glorious*
>
> *My colors grow brighter*
> *with the perfection of all that is*
> *in this moment*
> *in this world*
> *of constant change*
>
> *Time ebbs and flows with eternity*
> *but change is afoot*
> *it slows for no one*
> *and it celebrates itself*
> *whether we do or not*
>
> *I love change*
> *it makes me happy*
> *and completes all that must circle back to itself"*

- Julie shared that the Heart-leaf Buckwheat flower essence helped her "go with the flow" of change and gave her greater awareness about transitions.

- Cynthia took Heart-leaf Buckwheat during a time she felt like she was in a rut about her communication patterns. She was persistent and didn't want to give up or surrender her voice, but she knew something wasn't working so she was seeking answers and a new way to be.

- "The Heart-leaf Buckwheat flower essence felt highly stimulating to my 6th chakra and eyelids. My ears warmed, and then I felt a deep overwhelming nostalgic memory in my heart. I felt weepy at the memory of the crocuses that grew in my yard before I moved," Nikol shared. "The spirit of the plant feels like a large hand in front of my heart that I can fall forward into… and be held."

Meet Heart-leaf Buckwheat at Cape Horn in July.

Larkspur
Delphinium nuttallianum
Affirmation of the Wildflower: "*I delight in my true voice*"
Element: Air

Children • Communication • Delight • Forgiveness • Leadership • Relationship • Self-expression • Self-worth • Sound Healing • Truth • Chakra 4 (heart), 5 (throat)

Balanced: leading with a delighted heart in fully expressive communication

Fairies of the Larkspur flower love to sing. The buds look like musical notes dancing in the sky. They want you to sing your heart's song. Larkspur can lead you to de-light if you follow new paths of communication and unleash your creative expression.

A magical bluish-purple wildflower, Larkspur is a flower linked with all forms of self-expression. If we look really close, some of the petals have charcoal and white shimmery stripes. The first affirmation we heard from the Devas of the wildflower was actually a tone, "*AHHHHHHH.*" This tone cleanses the heart.

The word *Delphinium* means *dolphin*. Dolphins love to communicate through sound! I feel drawn to tone and make sounds when I am with the flower. I want to sing songs of my heart and follow where it leads me and not be held back by others. Speaking our truth is like that. We can't be bothered by what others think or do. We must *lead* our own way. Use the flower essence to inspire these qualities and open new pathways of communication.

I have given Larkspur to a number of clients to clear their throat chakra. It opened their sense of self and gave them a greater sense of freedom to speak clearly and ask for what they want. Often its affects are immediate.

Larkspur infuses us with magical and playful energies to instigate greater creative self-expression. As I write this description, I can feel Larkspur jumping off the page and wanting to engage with all of us. Feel free to do that. Invite the choir of Larkspur fairies in and they will come. They will help us find our voices… and sing out with us.

*"A free Soul
alights on tree-tops
carrying with it a
firm regard for delightful interactions.
How do you communicate best?
Why don't we try something
new*

*Renew your vows of friendship
with song and verse*

*Medleys and melodies parade
over our tongues
Anxious to be
expressed
and played with*

*Opportunities for joy
await us around
every corner
every tree
every flower*

*Visit us often
We will lead you to de-light"*

• Maureen felt an overall increase in energy after taking Larkspur flower essence, "I experienced the feeling of forgiveness which brought about a sense of joy."

• During a flower essence workshop, Sommer received a sweet little song from the Deva of Larkspur:

> *"I am the Larkspur of the Meadow x2*
> *And I bring you Grace, and I bring you home to Grace.*
>
> *I am the Voice of Violet Sunlight x2*
> *And I bring you home to Grace, and I bring you home to Grace*
>
> *I am the Song of Silent Thunder x2*
> *Growing Purple, Flowing Space*
> *Flowing Purple, Growing Space"*

- Abby shared her experience. "I took one drop of Larkspur and I immediately had this vision from Aladdin where the genie came out of the golden tea pot after being locked away for years and years. It was like my most pure, genuine form was set free with a loud, boisterous voice, holding back no inhibitions. It felt incredibly liberating and silly with this weight being lifted from holding myself captive."

- "Here's the dream I had after I took Larkspur one night and asked it for a dream." Saliha wrote, "I'm with a friend who is telling me that she has no plans for the future: i.e. 'in two years' time I want to be doing ____ or have accomplished ____.' When she says this, I realize how vital it is to be doing this, for example, 'in two years' time, I want to have finished voice-weavings. Then I'm singing aloud a goofy song that I myself don't like—I think it sounds sing-song and silly. I feel I need to sing it aloud to get it off my chest to make room for something better. A young man who is listening jokes about the sing-songy-ness of the song with me, calling it 'Two Drums and a Bass,' as if it were a marching band tune. I laugh, but I'm kind of embarrassed."

Meet Larkspur at Catherine Creek in April.

Mock Orange
Philadelphus lewisii
Affirmation of the Wildflower: "I am one-of-a-kind"
Element: Air, Water

Authenticity • Emotional Balance • Feminine/Women • Creativity • Harmony • Inner-essence • Nourishment • Originality • Purification • Purpose • Self-expression • Selfhood • Self-image • Stubbornness • Chakra 2 (sacral)

Balanced: harmonious and healthy self-image and ability to nurture emotional health

Numerous delightful and sweetly fragrant white blossoms spill from this unique small tree. Her scent is like Neroli, Orange Blossoms. Mock Orange may seem like a wanna-be Orange Blossom, yet she teaches that there is no need to aspire to be like another when your originality is a gift to the world.

It's hard to believe this wild bushy tree carries such a profusion of heady, fragrant flowers that look like a halo of white protection surrounding her branches. Her wood is used to make arrows. She told me, "Our blossoms create a halo of spiritual connection if you stand under the blossoms and allow us to transfer our wisdom and nourishment to you."

The spirit of this plant is no wanna-be or *mock* anything. She's the real deal. Authentic. She thrives with a very clear self-identification. She knows who she is. And, says it like it is. "My being nature is free from ties of emotionality. I don't need it—the drama. Just let me be me in peace. Then I'm happy."

When emotions get bottled up inside, we don't feel well. Stuck emotions may surface in our communication and behaviors in unhealthy ways or create disease if held inside. Mock Orange flower essence is indicated when we repress or suppress our emotions. In addition, it will help those that feel depleted, or starved, from lack of receiving juicy feminine spiritual nourishment. This Devas wants to help us receive what we are missing and find renewal of our emotional health.

Using the flower essence strengthens awareness of our identity—who we are and how we can be ourselves. False-identities that result from childhood and cultural conditioning can unravel. Our unique essential *essence* is our gift. Like a flower, each one of us vibrates with a beautiful and unique frequency. The flower essence helps us blossom in our own truth and recognize our inner-beauty. More harmony is made available to *be* our feminine nature.

I took Mock Orange before bed so I could learn more about its medicine. I dreamed I killed someone! I woke up disturbed by my nightmare but got the message it was a metaphor for emotions trapped in my psyche that needed to be released. The dream revealed that when my emotions were pent up and stewing within, a violent eruption could result. My *releasing dream*, and another one a few days later, gave me an opportunity to shed deep repressed emotions through the dreamtime. I also noticed my desire to be more honest in my communication with others about what worked for me and what didn't.

• Heather took some Mock Orange flower essence and immediately felt her heart blooming with love. As she continued taking the essence she felt a stillness and peace and the ability to step out and let her *stories* dissipate. She wrote, "The Deva is helping me trust and not be afraid to look at my emotions knowing my core is sweet and beautiful."

• Ellie didn't fit in anywhere as a child. She didn't resonate with anything that was mirrored back to her. She tuned into the idea that Mock Orange was about *Unity Through Diversity*—a world where we could honor and cherish our differences. She added, "Wouldn't that be amazing!" She always tells her son: "You are perfect the way you came in."

Ellie wrote, "In regards to Mock Orange and releasing of a relationship, I needed a knowing of who I am in my own uniqueness. What I released was the drama and expectation of others which is sometimes hard to do when there is an emotional connection. We feel responsible for the other person's happiness or experience. It clouds our own perception of our true nature. I was ready to let go of other's judgements about me, because I know I am my own unique, radiant being and that in itself is enough. Until I found my own center, though, I was often affected by how other people close to me felt. Mock Orange flower essence helps with self-image in this way, so that one can feel comfortable in one's own skin."

Meet Mock Orange at Hood River Mountain Meadow Trail in June.

Moss

Affirmation of Moss: "Nature hugs me with her love"
Element: Water, Earth

Abundance • Ancestor Healing DNA • Boundaries • Calming • Cellular Nourishment • Energetic Buffer • Premature Babies • Protection • Renewal • Chakra 4 (heart), 7 (crown)

Balanced: receptive to cellular nourishment of nature's soft, loving, and abundant renewal

Moss hugs the earth, trees, stones, and your own body like a calming protective energy buffer insulating you from life's intensities. Let its water seep into your skin to receive the deep cellular nourishment of mossious light and love. Make space for renewal… preferably a moss bed.

Moss is a holy substance of earth and water blended into a vibrant spongy, green soft carpet—the earth's magic carpet. It invites us to feel the moist earth and delight in the natural covering that caresses our senses and reminds us of nature's hugs. Moss hugs the earth, moss hugs trees, moss hugs rocks, moss hugs roofs and buildings and walkways in moist climates. It covers everything and extends its antenna into the space it occupies to perceive the world. It is abundantly present in the Pacific Northwest.

The plant spirit of Moss showed up when I was creating a flower essence blend for DNA healing and activation. I discovered that it is deeply nourishing for our cells and moss essence can affect change in our DNA. I believe in the power to activate and repair our DNA through shamanic, spiritual, and vibrational means. Vibrational energy medicine treats our energy body by repairing lapses in our subtle energy field and re-aligning new energetic pathways.

The essence of Moss is helpful for calming. It offers a feeling of protection for sensitivity. Moss creates a beautiful energetic buffer for extremely sensitive souls. I've noticed this fact after two of my apprentices shared that they were premature babies at birth. Moss really spoke to both of them. Both women were very psychically and energetically open. Moss seemed to add a layer of energy like a buffer to act as an additional filter for energies around them. When we need a protective hug, taking Moss essence nurtures us with Earth Mother's loving essence.

- Ellie speaks lovingly of moss as a sacred holder of water that cradles her. She feels instant tenderness when approaching and hugging moss covered trees. During fire ceremony, I soaked moss in the sacred ceremonially blessed water from around the world and bathed her feet as a blessing. I laid the moss on Ellie's feet and toes and held them. Ellie was transformed as she was infused with endearing love and energy from the essence of moss.

- Bonnie wrote: "Moss essence is my most favorite essence of all. It helps me feel more at home in the world this day and age when I quite frankly do not feel 'wired' for these times. There is a lot going on in our world today that I feel concerned about or wish were different which can feel very troubling. Moss helps me feel more resilient so I do not feel like I might crush under the weight of such collective heaviness. I find it comforting and fortifying for frayed nerves like restorative rest or a day spent recharging in Nature. It lends a seeming softness to the sharp edges of life to me."

- Katie S. shared, "When Camilla held space for a day-long class on connecting with home and land, I pulled the Moss card [Sacred Spirit Deck] which read, 'Nature hugs me with her love!' I really connected with that message so I asked for my own Moss Essence to work with at the end of class. When I took the essence, I immediately felt as though a large green loving being was gently holding me in their arms. I felt comforted, held, accepted and cherished. I take Moss essence when I feel stressed or ungrounded and it helps me experience grounding presence, self-love, acceptance and comfort."

Meet Moss on Wachlella Falls Trail.

Mt Hood (Wy'east)

Affirmation of Place: "I ground and align with the crystalline grid of the mountain"

Balanced: joyfully grounded in oneness with earth's elemental power

The mountain spirit holds high altitude divine consciousness and anchors it back on earth for grounding and stabilization. This mountain is quite young and active—a catalyst. I had a vision from high on Mt. Hood of many points of light or flowers. As each flower grew in power, its light radiated out more and more. All flowers of light connected together to form a grid. The grid was growing brighter and brighter with more and more flowers lighting up the planet. Align with the mountain to blossom with light.

As we choose, through intention, to be connected to the earth's body, our life becomes supported in all different ways. Our energy becomes one; we do everything together. The Crystalline Grid is like the nervous system of the planet and responds and flows through all crystalline forms—water, crystals, rocks, and mountains… and us humans. Our nervous system wants to be connected with The Crystalline Grid to give us stability and energy alignment. Just ask and it is so.

During the ascension process of earth, our bodies are transforming from carbon-based to crystalline structure. Like the earth or a crystal, we broadcast energy, transmit healing, send messages and communicate through our crystalline body the same way a mountain or a quartz crystal communicates through this vast invisible network of light. Our power as a source of light strengthens with our intentions.

Wy'east (Multnomah name for the mountain) is a powerful young and active mountain spirit that can bring us the deep grounding, earth connection, and stabilization we need to soar to new co-creative and spiritual heights. We can have a relationship with a mountain spirit by asking for a heart-connection and then spending time building this bond through direct experiences and intention.

My friend, Nance, and I hiked up to source waters high on the mountain a few years after the 9/11 tragedy. Our presence and intention to be of service helped open powerful channels of energy between Mt Hood and Ground Zero in Manhattan. Often, I visualize the mountain connecting with area mountains and mountaintops around the world through linking channels of light energy. I feel the power of this mountain connectivity and see that each one of us supports each other's blossoming evolution by connecting with each other and the mountains in this grid of love.

Mt Hood essence of place was co-created in connection with the purple heart of the mountain spirit and anchors our spirit into our body for strength of purpose. It helps us connect with the Crystalline Grid for grounding, stabilization, and communication with all of Creation. In this process, we are able to gently release feelings of separation from source and radiate our far-reaching light.

Mt Hood Lily
Lillium Cascadia
Affirmation of The Wildflower: "I claim my divine beauty and space"
Element: Water

Aura Repair • Beauty • Boundaries • Purification • Compassion • Creativity • Embodiment • Empowerment • Feminine/Women • Grief • Personal Space • Pregnancy • Purification • Purpose • Receptivity • Relationships • Self-image • Self-worth • Sensitivity • Sexuality • Shame • Stress • Surrender • Trust • Chakra 2 (sacral), 4 (heart)

Balanced: reclaiming expansive personal space that honors our creative nature

This pure white wild lily knows how to take up space and claim her full beauty and worth. Her tall height and delicious fragrance surprise those who find her in the forest. She reminds you to align with your pure divine essence and live large from this place. Claim sacred creative space for yourself. Lots of it!

I was enchanted on first sight of Mt. Hood Lily. Her spirit had called me up to the mountain that day to find her—a tall fragrant lily in the forest. Where did she come from? Not many wild lilies, orchids, or even roses were this showy. I was reminded of a lily you'd find in a flower shop. Most of the time, I see her in her pure white form, but her petals turn pink and even red as she ages.

As a white lily, Mt. Hood Lily addresses lily-themes of honoring the sacred feminine, self-worth, emotional healing, grief, spiritual sensitivity, and claiming personal boundaries and space. As I connected with Mt. Hood Lily, I realized what a precious treasure she was. She was living large, taking up her personal space, and loving the fullness of her experience. Most lilies are smaller. Not Mt. Hood Lily! She seems to revel in growing tall and being beautiful.

In a culture where we are taught to shrink ourselves down and stay small, it's a pleasure to receive permission to live large... yet in a feminine way. Learning how to do that may be a new adventure for many. We may be more used to living large in a masculine way or watching others live in a way that we are not connected to. Reclaiming our self-worth leads to living with this fullness. Owning our creativity and expanding our aura to its natural healthy size means we are building our confidence and life-force energy.

Taking the flower essence of Mt. Hood Lily helps us claim our full creative space and celebrate it. Celebrate being a woman, or celebrate our inner-feminine. It brings awareness to the way we pull in our energy because of protective patterns of being sensitive. She allows for more understanding of how we can care for our sensitivity and what is needed to feel good in our expression and in our body. During a *Sacred Spirit Deck* reading, a woman drew the Mt. Lily card and admitted that her husband was gradually taking over all the rooms in their house including her art studio. It was time to reclaim her creative space.

• At the *Portland Plant Medicine Gathering*, an attendee to my class on the lily flower essences shared her experience of the Mt. Hood Lily. Emily was a dancer as child but always felt bigger than the other kids because of her body type. She shrunk her size down energetically to fit in and be like the other ballerinas. She felt like a sparrow. After she took a few drops of the essence, she told us that she expanded into her true size. She claimed her energetic space and felt like a bear. She's loved bears and felt her spirit animal was bear so she was so grateful to come back to her proper size and form. She was excited by the prospect of taking up space and filling up her energy body with her true self.

• Andrea was thrilled with her experience of taking Mt. Hood Lily. She claimed the lily essence gave her a sense of where her skin and body ended and the world outside began. She kept touching her arms and body as she explained that it felt like a new experience of boundaries for her that gave her a stronger sense of self in relation to others—separate but connected. It gave her a new perspective on how to sense herself in space to enhance her self-worth.

Meet Mt Hood Lily on Tamawanas Falls Trail (Mt Hood) in June.

Mullein

Verbascum Thapsus
Affirmation of the Wildflower: "*I am still in order to listen*"
Element: Fire, Air, Earth, Water, Ethers

Balance • Breathe • Children • Clairaudience • Communication • Confidence • Death/Dying • Hearing • Embodiment • Fairy-Nature Realms • Feminine/Masculine Balance • Exhaustion • Fear • Immunity • Intimacy • Intuition • Judgment • Leadership • Listening • Responsibility • Rites of Passage • Self-assertiveness • Self discipline • Self esteem • Self-love • Self-worth • Sexuality • Spiritual Guidance • Stress • Trauma • Trust • Worry • Chakra 3 (solar plexus), 4 (heart), 6 (3rd eye)

Balanced: equilibrium that comes from listening to our higher guidance

Are you willing to sit with Mullein and listen to your own higher guidance? This plant can help you align with the cycles of your own personal power. The plant grows fuzzy soft leaves the first year and a tall, strong flowering stalk the second year. Mullein can balance yin and yang, help you honor the breath, and support community endeavors especially if everyone calls on the plant for assistance.

If I were a small fairy, I'd sleep in the soft, fuzzy Mullein leaves that circle in a cozy rosette pattern of the young plant. A very different plant emerges the second year. Out of this beautiful feminine softness grows a very tall and sturdy stalk of green. The torch, also called *witch's torch*, reaches for the heavens and soon is covered with small yellow flowers. Mullein's combination of feminine and masculine signatures help balance our yin and yang energy.

The plant grows and replenishes disturbed roadsides and depleted soil. Often, it is ignored or pulled out as a weed… unless you know its great power. Herbalists let it reach full glory in their landscapes and gardens. As an herbal medicine, Mullein has numerous healing properties. Our lungs and breath respond to the strengthening medicine of its fuzzy leaves. It makes a wonderful tea. Yellow Mullein flowers soaked in olive oil are used medicinally for earaches.

One of my first plant spirit experiences was during a meditation at a Reiki Circle. I had a vision of Mullein floating above my head like a holy presence or angel that came to assist me in my life. I followed the plant spirit. In another vision, I was carrying a burning torch made from a dried Mullein flower stalk leading the way in the dark. It was showing me how to keep moving like a light in the dark making a way for myself and others. The spirit of Mullein has been a beautiful ally for me over the years as a balancer and strengthener of my core self as it helped me deepen my commitment to my life and path. One day I was walking by Mullein and it spoke: *see with the eyes of your heart*. A Native American I met in Sedona said it is a very powerful plant and they use Mullein for the breath.

As a flower essence, Mullein can affect our sense of balance and equilibrium or inner-ear. Receptivity is enhanced. When we are willing to slow down and listen to our inner-guidance, balance is restored. Mullein has also been used for healing sexual abuse by opening and improving dialog between men and women.

Plants that grow a stalk with a strong vertical stem serve to enhance and strengthen our individuality and masculine virility. The stalk strengthens and aligns our backbone with life-force energy and purpose. Mullein frees fear of commitment by building courage. It can help us align with our cycles of power and commitment especially those with two-year cycles. It is helpful for projects or processes that need focused attention, discipline, and the ability to listen well working with others.

Two-year cycles can be supported with Mullein—projects, growth cycles. In the book, *Flower Essences and Vibrational Medicine*, Gurudas suggests taking Mullein in two stages. An essence from the first-year growth "creates a vortex of energy that brings people together." The second-year stalk and flowers "helps individuals or groups maintain momentum, persistence, and clarity of thought necessary to complete projects."

• Niki used Mullein during a time she was developing a shared vision for a new business venture and negotiating this exciting but scary territory. She ultimately decided to choose a different path and was highly successful because she listened to her guidance.

• Helen finds Mullein to be the mirror of perfect yin and yang balance. She uses it to open communication between her masculine and feminine energies so they are kept in balance. As a healing practitioner, she offers unique healing work. She tunes into the Mullein plant spirit through the flower essence and asks it to adjust the session if it is too yin or too yang.

Meet Mullein along roadsides of The Gorge in June and July.

Multnomah Falls

Affirmation of Water Place: "I am the pure and precious essence of love"

Balanced: wealth of overarching unconditional love and abundance

People travel from all over the world to see Multnomah Falls because of its height, beauty, and mystique. The waterfall occupies the place of *Mother* waterfall for the region as she envelopes all in her love and care. Your gratitude honors water's eternally giving nature and helps the spirit of Multnomah Falls purify, bless, and cleanse the land.

Even amongst crowds, Multnomah Falls is a great place to visit. Everyone is always happy. I see much love and joy shared in every group and family. A woman mothering her grandson swaddled in a white blanket whispered "it's so relaxing." The cave whispers, "serenity." Multnomah Falls carries the energy of unconditional love.

The energy field of Multnomah Falls reaches out to encompass a very large area that includes all the waterfalls in the Columbia River Gorge. The two waterfalls together rise 620 feet and are fed year-round by an underground spring. She is a central pillar of love—the *Mother* waterfall. She honors a golden love of humanity—all people, all colors, all nationalities. I've been intrigued by a Native American legend of the falls that tells of an Indian chief's beautiful daughter who sacrificed her life by leaping into the falls for the wellness of her people. There is a rock that represents her. Somehow, I couldn't find the resonance in this legend. In 1995, the huge 400-ton rock fell off the face of the falls and landed near a wedding party. Luckily, only minor injuries were reported. When the rock fell, the legend seemed to go with it. It makes sense that it's time for a new story—there is no need for women to sacrifice themselves to save others. We need healthy daughters, sisters, mothers, aunties, and grandmothers and their rich rivers of unconditional love to be strong.

Years ago, I had a visionary experience that changed the way I look at

Multnomah Falls. I was relaxing at the banks of the creek below the falls. As I moved into an altered state, I was given a large gold key. I was guided to place the golden key under the bridge into the lower falls and *unlock* an etheric door. I did. A doorway opened and a huge stream of intense liquid gold came pouring out. With my spiritual sight, I saw golden energy flow down the large waterfall, into the smaller one, into the creek, and finally merge with the liquid white water of the Columbia River. The liquid gold felt like unconditional love—thick and full of substance—yet only visible through spiritual sight. I felt a bit overwhelmed at this display of love and flowing abundance. I was told, "The Columbia River is a vein of golden consciousness for the earth." I was humbled by my experience and grateful at the opportunity to be of service. A brilliant rainbow appeared in the water as I left the falls that day.

When I tune into the spirit of water, I usually sense or feel feminine Devas or elementals of the water—mermaids, undines, fairies, Goddesses, Grandmothers, water serpents or dragons, salmon, whales, turtles, or dolphins. Multnomah Falls came in as a Rainbow Mother Goddess. She carries an aspect of Mother Earth and wants to ground us in our power so we know our self-worth—our preciousness. A message came in…

> *"The healing of the whole world can come through the love of the Mother. My waters help you honor the mother, become receptive to her love including the love of Mother Earth for us, her children. She calls out to us to receive her love, comfort, and grace.*
>
> *Mother Earth is the pot of gold—the abundance that we seek and the precious gold, riches, and wealth of love we seek. Love is the true wealth we seek."*

Multnomah Falls essence of place imbues us with the golden consciousness of unconditional love. The Rainbow Mother Goddess of Multnomah Falls wants us to live in a state of gratitude for the feminine spirit of water and for the waters that run through our veins—our blood. Water is precious. Our own waters are precious. Receive her love to create a wealthy life.

Ocean Spray
Holodiscus discolor
Affirmation of the Wildflower: "I flow with grace"
Element: Water

Abundance • Beauty • Childbirth • Children • Channeling • Clairsentience • Creativity • Embodiment • Exercise • Flow • Feminine/Women • Guilt • Heart Healing • Intuition • Joy • Rhythm • Self-expression • Self-image • Sensitivity • Sexuality/Sensuality • Shame • Shadow Aspect • Chakra 2 (sacral)

Balanced: an abundant and continuously flowing, dancing, and openly embodied state

These flowers spray their foaming sweet blossoms like waves in the wind. The energy of Ocean Spray is like a Goddess that answers to the rhythm of nature to balance the flow of your feminine (or inner-feminine) cycles. Ask the flower spirit to align you with healthy natural rhythms and cycles so everything can flow with ease.

Overflowing with an abundance of white blossoms, Ocean Spray grows by the moist ocean as well as inland in Oregon and Washington. Its flowers look like an explosion of foamy water and spray that is coming off the ocean waves hence its name. The large bushes usually burst with a profusion of fragrant blooms in June. The plants color the forests with their graceful elegance and soft scent.

Danu, the Fairy Queen often appears to me when I take the Ocean Spray flower essence. She takes me on an ethereal and sensual journey of joy. She says that Ocean Spray is a divine flower of movement and joy. Ocean Spray dances with possibilities for greater openings and is a good *channeler's* flower. Ocean Spray gets energy flowing in and out of the 2nd chakra—emotional power center and place of abundance, pleasure, sexuality, relationship, and creativity. This chakra loves the flowing energy of water and with it the movement that cleanses and refreshes and moves congestion in the body.

This flower essence helps us flow more easily with our body's ability to sense and feel through our 2nd chakra, the pelvis and sacral area. Ocean Spray connects us to the natural flow of energy and information that is available to guide us if we listen to our body and our clairsentience (clear feeling). It also helps us become more aware of synchronistic occurrences and receptive inflows of magical energy. Embracing our feelings and emotions helps us find our rhythm and flow.

Many of my students who have used Ocean Spray say they experienced themselves as "going with the flow" more easily and looking at things with a new perspective. One student was feeling the discomfort of not knowing which way to flow so she welcomed Ocean Spray's wisdom and sense of gentle direction.

• Angela was born in the astrological sign of Cancer, a water sign. She said that Ocean Spray really helped her keep her energy flowing. The way she flowed was also more directed like she had banks for her river of energy instead of flowing all over the place and diluting her energy. Also, Angela didn't have to rely on combative energy to create boundaries. She felt smoother, calmer, and more clearly directed taking the flower essence.

• After using Ocean Spray flower essence, Maureen said, "Wow! I felt a complete freeing of my emotions—laughter, crying, etc. Which lead to feelings of lightness and joy."

• Joanna used Ocean Spray during the water birth of her daughter to keep labor flowing. She took drops internally and added them to the birth tub. The birth flowed beautifully.

Meet Ocean Spray at Mayer State Park in June.

Oregon Grape
Berberis aquifolium
Affirmation of the Wildflower: "I trust in myself"
Element: Fire

Abandonment • Anxiety • Attachment • Children • Compassion • Defensiveness • Energy Blocks/Flow • Heart Healing • Judgement • Loneliness • Performance Anxiety • Protection • Self-expression • Trust • Vulnerability • Chakra 1 (root), 3 (solar plexus), 4 (heart)

Balanced: trusting, vulnerable, and undefended in relationships

The barbed leaves of Oregon Grape are prickly like holly, the berries are mouth-puckering sour and tart, yet the yellow blossoms are so sweetly scented and appear so trusting, vulnerable, and undefended. The state flower of Oregon populates wide areas in The Columbia River Gorge. You'll never feel lonely if you befriend this plant.

Even when we are attracted to the exotic, our best medicine is often the common native plant that grows outside our door. I've lived near beloved Oregon Grape for years. I respect this plant. Its leaves will prick you if you don't. And, I am drawn to touch its shiny leaves, smell its yellow flowers, and gobble up its hardy tart berries whenever I see them. I feel like I am inviting its spirit to dance with me when I do.

When I first made the Oregon Grape flower essence I heard the song, "The Great Pretender." In the song, he sings about 'pretending I'm doing well… and I'm lonely but no one can tell. … pretending you're still around." I take this as a hint to indicate who will benefit from using the flower essence. It can help those who feel a sense of abandonment but may not want to admit it. Or, feel loneliness and cover up their feelings too well.

As a fruiting plant, the flower essence of Oregon Grape is very nourishing. It addresses trust issues, misconceptions, and mistaken beliefs about ourselves that can create negative thinking and defensive behavior. Sometimes we fear vulnerability or that we will be hurt or abandoned once again. We may feel overly protective or walled off. Our beliefs create further entanglements that continue our patterns. We believe what is not really true. What beliefs hold us back? This flower opens our awareness and helps build trust.

"It's easy to distract yourself from how you're feeling
there is plenty of busyness in the world
but I will help you sink deeper
into yourself and find the place
that is calling to your soul

Yes, I can help your focus… on what's really important
what your heart cries out for
attune to your right livelihood, your calling
your true love

A lot of people feel burdened when they don't have to be
The burdens are self-imposed and are created by incorrect beliefs
I can help you rid the erroneous judgments—free up more space

Focus
Put your heart on the line"

• Tom had recently moved to Oregon and needed a flower essences to integrate different aspects of his life. He wanted to feel good about living in a city without having to feel so defended all the time. He used Oregon Grape flower essence as his support.

• One of Herbalist Jeff's favorite plants is Oregon Grape. He likes this plant because it offers him strength and protection and a sense of being loved and connected to all of Creation. It supports him and addresses his issue of abandonment.

• Darlene (not her real name) wrote, "Oregon Grape helped me become okay with not always knowing exactly how things might turn out. It allowed me to relax into the flow of life and to begin to experience joy I hadn't felt since childhood. It helped me begin to trust in myself again, with a newfound confidence, that didn't come from achievements or belief systems, but from a deep connection between me and the web of life."

• Katie S. wrote, "The essence of Oregon Grape helps me release that which is not mine and assists me to let go of responsibility for other people's feelings. It guides me back to my own power and center. This flower essence was very helpful at the end of a relationship to restore my energy and release the other person's energy. This song comes through when I work with plant essence:

> *"In this sacred forest, I remember who I am*
> *Mahonia Mahonia bringing me home again*
> *In this sacred boundary I am strong I purify*
> *Mahonia Mahonia bringing me home again*
> *Now I know the truth of what is yours and what is mine!*
> *Mahonia Mahonia bringing me home again"*

Meet Oregon Grape on Hamilton Mountain Trail in May.

Oregon Oak

Quercus garryanna
Affirmation of the Tree: "I am strong in purpose & joy"
Element: Earth

Ancestor Healing • Boundaries • Courage • Detoxification • Defensiveness • Focus • Grounding • Immunity • Inner-Strength • Intuition • Masculine Principle • Nervous System • Patience • Protection • Purpose • Receptivity • Responsibility • Safety • Security • Self-discipline • Support • Strength • Stress • Surrender • Trust • Worry • All Chakras

Balanced: joyful yielding to true meaning of strength; knowing true purpose is supported

Lean against an Oregon Oak tree to remember the need to yield to the strength of others at times. The Oregon Oak supports a great number of beings in its branches. If you support many others, you may see yourself in the Oregon Oak. If you feel joy, then this is your purpose. If not, then lean into the Oak.

Oak is revered as the sacred *Tree of Life* to the Celts of Northern European lineage. The Celtic word for Oak is *daur* which is the origin of the word *door*. Oaks are the *axis mundi*, the center of the world, and the doorway to the *Otherworld*, the realms of Fairy. In Celtic Shamanism, trees are considered elders, ancestors, guardians of wells, healers, and entry to the supernatural world.

Oaks are magical trees that often create groves or circles of energy. I have been blessed to live inside circles of Oregon White Oak trees for almost twenty years at three different houses. Rough silvery gray bark and freeform branches shaped by the elements animate the tree. The Oak's presence is very grounding and secure but also surprisingly gentle and loving. They are drought tolerant and depend on disturbance to take root.

The many beings that live in and with Oak like to share their strength and magic with others, too. Squirrels have a special love for Oaks and their fruit—acorns. Lichen, woodpeckers, tanager, snakes, mistletoe, wasp-created galls, fairies, gnomes, moss, and many other inhabitants use the tree as their home base or hub. Some kinds of Trilliums need their shelter.

For human Oak-types, there are times that call for yielding and receiving of support especially when trying to be too strong for everyone else. I have seen strong Oaks fall. In order to be a balanced forest-dweller we must be willing to be supported by other trees. Our strength and sense of responsibility must be tempered with joy and time for play. Fathers, mothers, and those that struggle or tend to over-work can align deeper with their purpose and a more supportive life. Now is the time for effortlessness. Inner-strength means we can stand still and be with one's self.

Oregon Oak flower essence comes from a catkin flower of the native tree and helps us see ourselves as strong. It balances and refines our sense of duty. When we are trying too hard, overtaxing our energy, or focusing on goals and our to-do list, Oak can help us find greater balance. After we find our *true* sense of strength, we can relax more.

> *"Strength refined*
> *stand tall in your splendor*
> *be still in joy*
> *choose to remember your nature*
>
> *Time has cast its*
> *net over you*
> *keeping you tied to the past,*
> *the future, and striving ways*
>
> *Learning to share in the*
> *heartspace of eternity*
> *will bring you much more joy*
>
> *Exceptional experiences*
> *resonate with the highest*
> *frequencies of pleasure*

work-share-joy-purpose
all matter if your
passion plays

Why not agree to trying
new attitudes of believing
Trusting not the purpose
as a whole but as an
essence of your presence

Find Oneness in believing
we all stand tall together
Trees and humans in a forest of love"

- Glen was brought to tears when he felt the Oregon Oak tree support *him*. He sensed that he didn't have to hold so much strength for his two young daughters and wife and as teacher and naturopathic doctor because the tree would support him with *its* strength.

- Maureen immediately felt grounded, stable and very connected to earth. "It also brought me a wonderful sense of fullness and calm."

- Jackie felt the Oregon Oak essence surround her with a beautiful masculine protective strength so she could open and trust and allow her feminine energies to be more fully expressed.

Meet Oregon Oak throughout The Gorge especially Pine-Oak Woodlands (near Mosier, OR or Lyle, WA).

Phantom Orchid

Cephalanthera austiniae
Affirmation of the Wildflower: "*I remove all blocks and interference*"
Element: Water, Air

Aura Repair • Catalyst • Children • Courage • Detoxification • Energy Blocks • Enlightenment • Flow • Forgiveness • Fear • Grounding • Guilt • Illusion • Immunity • Pain • Purification • Resentment • Shadow Aspect • Sexuality • Stress • Transformation • Transition • Truth • Worry • Chakra 2 (sacral), 4 (heart), 7 (crown)

Balanced: walking with the light of Truth free of illusionary patterns

The pure white Phantom Orchid appears as if it is a lantern shining brightly in the dark forest. One word came from its lips: *illusion*. The lantern lights the way towards Truth… if you are willing.

The dark forest felt mysteriously intense as we entered in broad daylight. Soon we saw the pure white Phantom Orchids glowing bright like lanterns in the darkness. I was awed by its mystery. I am reminded of the a wise guide who carries a light to guide the way—not afraid to follow the sacred path alone. I moved closer to smell the flower; it smelled faintly like vanilla. The flowers are small and white with a touch of yellow growing on a waxy white stem. It contains no chlorophyll so it can't feed itself. It feeds off dead matter in the soil. This wild, native Northwest orchid offers strong gifts through its essence.

The Phantom Orchid flower essence is a master cleanser, purifier, and seeker of Truth. Use it to clear energy and to move obstacles, interference, or blocks. The Phantom Orchid lights up what is dark or denied within us. I have often seen the flower addressing the very deepest core for clients. Orchids can be cathartic for those who are very sensitive to energy and need it most.

"Holding Truth requires purification
Clear the clutter
Get everything out of the way
It's time for Truth
Shifting into Truth
is ascension
No illusion will last for long
There is a calm that holds firm when you are there—in Truth
Great clouds of substance
Separating fact from fiction can be fun
Who's the phantom now?"

I gave my client, Mary, a few drops of Phantom Orchid flower essence before an energy healing session. Soon after, she was surprised to feel the presence of the plant spirit in the room. It swept her energy body clean of a cloud of old energies even before we began our session.

• A Portland acupuncturist uses Phantom Orchid for pain. He places drops on his patient's body for immediate pain relief.

• "Phantom Orchid is one of my favorites to work with as a massage practitioner. Many times, clients had a knot [tight muscles] that I couldn't seem to work out and I'd put a drop or two of Phantom Orchid on the spot and the knot released immediately," Jannine wrote.

• Working with Phantom Orchid, Lorca started questioning everything including her expectations. "It was a revelation, my shadow. I needed to look at everything, revisit, reevaluate. It was not easy, but it moved me to a better place. I even *saw* eyes asking 'Who are we?' And I recognized who I am!"

Meet Phantom Orchid on Herman Creek Trail in May.

Poet's Shooting Star
Dodecatheon poeticum
Affirmation of the Wildflower: "I am fully present"
Element: Air, Earth

Acceptance • Autism • Astrology • Belonging • Children • Detoxification • Earth Mother Connection • Fairy-Nature Realms • Grounded • Homesickness • Now • Star-seed • Uplifting • Chakra 1 (root)

Balanced: sense of belonging on earth, here and now, in joyful communion with the stars

This beautiful flower points downward to the earth. The healing signature of downward pointing plants represents embodiment issues. The wildflower points to where you landed, where you belong, your home. Poet's Shooting Star helps you bring your full attention and focus into being here, now, in your body.

Poet's Shooting Star is sweet and magical and colorful—dark pink, yellow, and white form intricate colored patterns etched with black geometric patterns. The black tip points down towards the ground as its delicate pink petals flare back like wings. This flower was my son's favorite. It has a very fun, playful, and grounding nature—full of sunshine and magic. It says, "It's not about going someone else… it's here." It seems to resonate with poets, astrologers, children, our inner-child, and the highly sensitive *starseed* types. *Starseeds* feel like they come from another planet.

The flower helps us feel more fully present in every moment and in our earthly life. We belong here. It helps us integrate our spiritual, mental and emotional selves into our physical body so we can shine more brightly. It aids the process of bringing our focus and full attention into all that we are and all that we do, now. Poet's Shooting Star assists *starseed* children, or others, that feel they've come from cosmic origins and find being on Earth confusing and challenging. It assists those who find difficulty in being grounded or finding a sense of belonging. It can also soothe and heal birth trauma or disconnection we may have experienced from the way we were born. Our birth can set up life-long patterns or a sense of homesickness—wanting to return *home* or to the stars.

While making the Poet's Shooting Star essence, I felt a strong presence of my *inner-starchild*—the part of me that was anxiously awaiting attention. My *star-child* wanted me, and others, to know that they can guide us in new ways in this expanding universe. They want to be in communication. To cure homesickness or awaken an understanding of our relationship to the celestial realms, we can invite this part of ourselves in and listen to their starry wisdom. On another day, the flower shared the words *play, create, inspire, dance*, and *remember*. Root in. Presence is key.

According to Gurudas in *Flower Essences and Vibrational Medicine*, astrologers can heighten their understanding and intuition of the planets, including earth using this essence. Shooting Star protects us against most environmental pollutants. It strengthens all meridians and magnifies all chakras.

• Robbie said, "While taking the essence, I am landed, grounded, and brilliant just like the flower! I see that the way I was living was from the *outside in* and now being present to myself from the *inside out* is a whole new reality that is much more honoring."

• Niki, a young woman very attuned to working with children and animals came in for a healing session. She tested for Poet's Shooting Star during the session. Afterwards, she told me that her friend had written her a poem the previous day describing her like a "shooting star." She was having issues about being more grounded in her body and feeling like she had no roots in Oregon as she had recently moved from Hawaii. She didn't feel she belonged here until she took the flower essence.

• Laura J. found Poet's Shooting Star flower essence grounded her so deeply her thoughts and even sensations were absent. It gave her a sense of home. "Home can be anywhere and everywhere."

• Cindy told me she still didn't feel like she was *back* from a recent vacation. On the flight, she was hit on the head with a piece of luggage. I gave her a few drops of Poet's Shooting Star. Immediately, we both felt her spirit return to her body. "Now I'm home," she said. She began using this essence and it seemed to always have a strong way of returning Cindy to her body to balance her beautiful expanded spiritual presence in a more grounded way.

• Ellie O. felt very present. She noticed the French song in the background of the Tea Lounge: "I don't want to work today." It mirrored her sentiment exactly. She wasn't keen on applying for a job. But she heard the spirit of the flower speak. "You are ready to move on in your life and become a professional working woman." She saw a shield form over her aura and felt strong in it. The fairies took her to a lake and dolled her up and made her *professional-looking* for job interviews. The shield felt very present and grounding. "I was shiny. They told me how incredible I'd be, that I'll be needed, and how patient I've been. Get going! How beautiful you are!" Flowers were shining out of my aura. Ellie added, "Who would've thought that flowers could be my guides."

Meet Poet's Shooting Star at Cherry Orchard Trail in April.

Ponderosa Pine
Pinus ponderosa
Affirmation of the Tree: "*I trust all is well*"
Element: Fire, Earth, Air

Acceptance • Anger • Emotional Balance • Emotional Telepathy • Feeling Nature • Guilt • Identity • Inner-Child • Innocence • Judgement • Meditation • Peace • Protection • Self-blame • Self-care • Sensitivity • Shame • Silence • Strength • Touch • Trust • Vulnerability • Witness • Chakra 2 (sacral), 4 (heart)

Balanced: strong in inner-peace and self-acceptance

Tall and silent guardians of The Gorge thrive in the heat and fire of the sun. Ponderosa Pine offers a deep-felt sense of innocence, peace, and trust in life. They hold a gentle, caring power. The bark smells like vanilla and appears as puzzle pieces. When it's time for the pieces of your life to come together, sit with this tree.

Ponderosa Pine carries a strong and pure spirit as it soars tall in silence, but when the wind blows it dances and sings with life. The coloring and forming of the bark always seems inexplicably beautiful— reddish, orange, brown and blackened puzzle pieces. It is fairly common to see trees blackened by lightning strikes. Heat intensified its sweet vanilla-like resinous fragrance. The tree helps us slow way down to receive its healing caresses—its touch.

Touchy-feely is a great way to describe the spirit of pine. I find them very sensitive beings and they appeal to that aspect of myself. Its pine needles, or leaves, form delightful tufts and boughs that attract our hands to touch, stroke, shake, brush them. When I find a pine bough, I instinctually use it to brush off my body to cleanse and fluff up my aura. When I am feeling a great need to be touched and held, Ponderosa helps me hold my own heart in the silence of love. This satisfies my need for physical touch, somewhat. In *Awakening to the Plant Kingdom* by Robert Shapiro and Julie Rapkin, a Pine tree speaks through a channeling: "We are very sensitive to touch… When we reach out into the world to broadcast messages to others of our species, our auric field gets very large and very sensitive. We will actually feel the fly heading in to land on us."

Where I live, Ponderosa Pine is a prominent and beloved tree. It offers a sublime and enduring sense of innocence and self-acceptance. Recently, I began weaving Ponderosa pine needle baskets. Something really profound happened as I gathered the long pine needles outside my door and soaked them overnight. Bending them and shaping them into a spiral to sew together with raffia, I added more of the needles with every few stitches. I began weaving my new life. I felt such peace sitting in the presence of huge guardian pine trees swaying gently with the wind. Their gratitude was palatable. And, I felt their love for me and the power of this connection.

Ponderosa Pine's guardian spirit creates sacred and gentle space—a space of non-judgment. Nothing we do is right or wrong, good or bad. There is no innocence or guilt. Everything just *is*. We can settle deeply within and sense the roots and origins of our own essential being in tune with all of Creation.

> *"I am the Pine Maiden and I came to you to give you a message. A message of love. We bring you warmth for your fire and needles for your baskets and peace in your being. We ask you to be in peace with us. We need your peace, too. It helps us be at peace within ourselves. We are linked this way—humans and trees—our need for each other. We want to stand with you like a forest of humans and trees holding hands and branches that connect our hearts and become one band. Our music is a band with many players. We whistle to hear you whistle. We listen for your songs and loving music. We want to play music with you and be at peace."*

Words are not the usual way I communicate with pine—I *feel* them and I believe they feel me too. They gift me with songs. They speak through the wind and in their silence but mostly through their feelings and emotional telepathy—using their hearts to connect in the *language of nature*. Pine brings out the sense of touch and how we truly feel deep down. Pine allows the vulnerability of our feelings when no one else can. The flower essence helps us be in this feeling state so we can let go of self-blame and restore our sense of innocence and self-acceptance.

• When Heather needed Ponderosa Pine, she saw the tree everywhere. Like a steady presence that kept reminding her that all is well when she balances play and rest, play and rest, and trust. The pine tree trunk gave her a steady place to sink into when she needed grounding. The pine needles inspires a song set to *"Shake your Bootie": Shake Shake Shake, Shake Shake Shake, Shake your pine needles, Shake your pine needles, I like the way you ground me, You make me feel so calm and steady."*

• Elyssa shared, "Ponderosa Pine and its essence presents itself to me as a mama bear. A dose goes right to my heart chakra, comforting, protecting, grounding, nourishing with the energy of a hug. Camilla and I first met at Catherine Creek by the Columbia River Gorge. We walked a beautiful trail and Camilla introduced me to the pine. I will never forget its bark: speckled and dragon like. I put my hand on the tree and journeyed into a space of protection—the bark wanted to armor me and ground me deep into my roots. The pine was a mama bear who let me know she would hold me with love and not let any outside influence disturb my peace. She taught me I had a fiercely loyal and loving protection for all of my sweetness. This pine holds my heart with a sense of safety—its beauty and mystery reminding me that the earth is full of wonder and grace and a depth that is nearly indescribable."

• Joanna H. shared, "Ponderosa Pine was my first experience taking a flower essence daily. I found the effects to be subtle, yet it has had a tangible influence on my emotional and mental state. Since taking it regularly, I have felt more grounded and stable, felt a deeper sense of strength within myself. My connection to nature, especially trees and plants has deepened. I have felt a gentle energetic shift overall that I have found to be very healing and beneficial in my daily life."

Meet Ponderosa Pine throughout The Gorge especially Pine-Oak Woodlands (near Mosier, Oregon or Lyle, WA).

Pungent Desert Parsley
Lomatium grayii
Affirmation of the Wildflower: "*I awaken to my true self*"
Element: Fire, Air

Astral Projection • Aura Repair • Authenticity • Balance • Boundaries • Channeling • Children • Happiness • Hypnotherapy • Illness • Immunity • Intuition • Masculine/Men • Mental Balance • Nervous System • Nourishment • Psychic Development • Relationships • Sensitivity • Sound Healing • Stress • Trust • Will • Chakra 3 (solar plexus), 4 (heart)

Balanced: a state of being that allows a gentle, subtle awareness and emergence of the true Self

The pungent scent of this wildflower wakes the senses and warms the body. Pungent Desert Parsley asks you to open your sensitivity as if you had antenna. Use this form of sensing to discover your world anew. What signals are you picking up?

The yellow Pungent Desert Parsley is called pungent because of its stimulating and unusually strong smell. It blooms in early spring with airy yellow pompom-like umbel flowers that spread over the intricate masses of bright green foliage. It loves rocky high ground.

As a flower essence, Pungent Desert Parsley teaches us how to *be*—without masks, pretense, or ego hiding our vulnerability. I saw a mask lying on the ground when I made the essence which revealed a need to release the way we hide ourselves. Our authentic self can emerge from deep nourished roots into the open air. Its gentle protective quality mirrors a teaching of how to be with ourselves in this gentle, simple, and open way. In the Native American tradition, the medicine of Deer is similar—learning how to be gentle, sensitive, and open. I had a vision of a deer leaping when I made this essence.

The essence works to repair our subtle relationship with masculinity and/or being a man as well as issues regarding our parent's preference for a boy at birth. It can strengthen our awareness about our boundaries in space and bring more air or lightness of being into what was heavier, darker, and rooted in non-truth. I have experienced how it can balance our protective auric field by quickly re-aligning the layers so we feel protected, whole, and clear. As a Parsley Family flower, it supports nervous system integration and integration of sensory input. It teaches us how to relax and allow the gentle unfolding of life.

• Stephanie's auric field was pulled over to the left side emphasizing her feminine-side. Pungent Desert Parsley worked quickly in re-aligning and re-balancing her energy field. Her aura shifted back to center, and she felt much clearer and more protected. She now had access to her full life-force and firmer sense of an auric boundary.

• Jill had been using the Pungent Desert Parsley for about 6-8 weeks for ongoing issues with being an energy sensitive person for years. She had been at a loss for how to maintain her own balance at times, psychically and emotionally. "The flower essence has been very helpful to me and most recently I have received more insight/guidance in how to actually transmute energies that I feel on the physical level. It is easier to find balance emotionally. It is such a relief."

Meet Pungent Desert Parsley at Catherine Creek in April.

Queen Bead Lily
Clintonia uniflora
Affirmation of the Wildflower: "I am a Queen of the Light"
Element: Water, Air, Earth

Ascension • Boundaries • Clearing • Compassion • Embodiment • Emotional Healing • Father Issues • Feminine/Women • Grace • Grief • Guilt • Incest • Purification • Sexual Abuse • Shame • Spiritual Nourishment • Self-worth • Chakra 2 (sacral), 4 (heart), 7 (crown)

Balanced: sense of purity and compassion for feminine embodiment

The Queen holds the power of purification for the feminine body, emotions, and Soul. Let her deep compassion and grace model a new form of power steeped in love, kindness, and truth. Follow her path of light through the forest on full moon nights to awaken your inner-Queen. Let the moon reflect your beauty, too.

When I returned from the Fairy Congress, I went up to Sahalie Falls on Mt. Hood and was overjoyed to see a whole stand of Queen Bead Lilies. I toned a new chant, "F-A-Y. I Love You. F-A-Y. I Love You." Before I could finish the third round, a hummingbird flew over and hovered inches in front of my face and looked into my eyes. After I looked back with a smile, it flew away. "F-A-Y. I Love You." Overjoyed with my fairy messenger, I sat with my Queen Bead Lilies. They whispered the word: *compassion*.

At another time, I heard her voice again: *we are for the sins of your fathers, incest*. This was unexpected as I don't often hear the flowers speak of such traumatic life challenges in such a direct way, and I did not have experience working with victims of abuse. Years later, I traveled across the western US with a Native American medicine man and we offered ancestor healing ceremony together. More times than not the client's healing (or her lineage) related to sexual abuse and incest. Queen Bead

Lily and the white lilies became an ally and healer for many women. The lily asked me to hold healing space for survivors of abuse and incest and generously offered her healing frequencies. My relationship with the spirit of Queen Bead Lily gave me the medicine that is needed for healing this heart-breaking trauma and accompanying guilt and shame.

I'll never forget my moonlit walk with the Queen Bead Lily on Larch Mt. She illuminated my path with her pure white reflective powers—six radial white petals and three thick leafs low on the forest floor. Lily, in her quiet feminine power, is like a lunar queen of the night. She shared her beauty and light so I could walk on… in the dark. Joy overflowed as I felt her sparkling breath and celebration of my sacred feminine nature. Lilies help us celebrate being women or the feminine nature.

I became so intrigued with my lily queen (also called Queen's Cup, Bride's Bonnet, Bead Lily) that I commissioned my fairy dressmaker friend, Sheri Trnka, to create an outfit for me. Fairy Congress was coming up and I wanted a flowering dress. She made me a Queen Bead Lily outfit. We had visited the woods together and seen their surprising fruit on a thin stem where the flower once grew—one slate blue magical bead (berry)—hence the name Queen Bead Lily. My green velour skirt had petals, the sleeveless inner shirt was white with threads forming leaf patterns, the green jacket had long white lily petals at the cusp of the sleeves and it fastened with a slate blue bead button. I felt like I embodied a lily when I wore it.

The lilies have always touched my emotional nature deeply. Lily bulbs are lightly rooted in the earth and hold water for the plant. The lilies help us move grief—our emotional waters. Grief may be buried within if we haven't given ourselves permission to express our intuitive feminine nature. In addition, as an essence from a fruit/berry plant, it is very energetically nourishing, like spiritual food.

During ancestor healing ceremony, I often connect with trapped earthbound spirits that need help moving to the light. A mother or grandmother in someone's lineage who experienced incest may have buried her secret or even been victimized further by speaking out. This trauma can affect their passing… and their daughters and granddaughters through the generations. To offer an ancestral remedy, I place a small bowl of water out for the ancestors and add a few drops of Queen Bead

Lily flower essence to the water with intention. I am truly amazed and delighted at the energetic shift I feel when I use the essence this way. The frequency of this energetic medicine moves through their etheric being and brings healing and awareness to the spirit.

- Sharon (not her real name) used Queen Bead Lily essence after an ancestor healing ceremony to nourish her being and keep her emotions flowing and releasing. Because of the trauma around childhood abuse, she said it felt emotionally intense at times. She felt grateful that the spirit of the flower really helped her stay present with herself and her body as an energetic support for her healing process.

- Sara M. told me she didn't feel a lot of energy taking the flower essence. I told her that lilies can be very subtle in their energy and affects. She paused and said she did notice that she was caring for herself more since she began taking Queen Bead Lily flower essence. In a few weeks, she wrote: "When we saw each other I had just used the Queen Bead Lily two times and just a few drops under my tongue. That afternoon I drank her in water and continued to for a week. This is how she really wanted me to take her in ... through water. Since then, I have cried more that I have in a very long time. Every day I am touched so deeply by something seemingly benign and I have tears. I actually stopped taking her after a week just to give a break ... I was feeling so so sad. Sad because of how mean people are to each other and themselves, deeply sad that strife seems to be felt more than kindness between people and groups of people. I was even sad for the current president! How he lives in and breeds so much self-importance and intolerance to life. It broke my heart that he lives in this way.

I will begin taking Queen Bead Lily flower essence again because I feel that I have only started to feel the tip of the iceberg of what this lady can do for my capacity to open. The tears have not stopped just the intensity. I also wonder if this is how the essences work: once a level of their work is done then that level is done and stays."

Right after receiving her description, I had a dream of Sara. I was seeing her beautiful lily nature—very sensitive, open, pure, feminine. I was observing the play of her gentle nature with me—I was in a different state of being. I saw how important it is to be clear with our words and boundaries to carry this refined lily energy in our world and stand firm in a gentle way. Sara does that well. The dream reminded me to be clear and firm with my boundaries in order to claim my own lily nature more.

Meet Queen Bead Lily in Larch Mt Forest in July.

Red Columbine
Aquilegia Formosa
Affirmation of the Wildflower: "*I free my will*"
Element: Fire

Alignment • Balance • City Living • Confidence • Disperse Geopathic Stress • Earth Changes • Electro-Magnetic Frequencies (EMFs) • Empowerment • Harmony • Intentionality • Manifestation • Receptivity • Self-expression • Sensitivity • Will • Chakra 3 (solar plexus)

Balanced: strength of will to act on own behalf to manifest desires and dreams

Receiving what you truly want is your birthright. Nature wants you to fulfill your desires, too. Your will is Divine will. Red Columbine helps you act from a place of knowing that you have the ability and confidence to create what you want and live out your dreams.

Red Columbine is an unusually shaped orangey-red and yellow beauty. Its stamens hang down and sway in the winds of The Gorge. The flower's shape is reminiscent of a jester's cap, a bonnet, or some kind of head ornamentation. My first instinct on meeting the wildflower was to imagine the flower stamens as electrical plugs that plugged in at the crown of my head. It was as if I was an electrical being and the flower was re-charging me from Source energy. Miraculously, when I first took the flower essence that is what happened. My electrical system re-aligned as if by magic. I could sense and feel the energy flow in my nervous system shift and flow into healthier alignment. I was quite surprised and delighted by my experience.

After that, I shared this flower essence with many others and even placed drops on people's heads. Red Columbine had the same effect on most everyone. Sometimes it was a strong energetic movement and others times it's subtle, but it always brought a greater sense of balance and clarity to the person. And, sometimes an element of surprise to be so aligned with their personal intentions.

As I've come to understand the flower's medicine, I see how much our beliefs and focus of our will—our personal intention and what we want and desire—shapes the energy flow in our bodies. I believe the flower helps us re-dedicate our energy so we can build our capacity to create dreams from within. Red Columbine tells us to empower our will—command what we truly desire! Bring confidence to our self-expression. It supports our self-sovereignty and ability to act on our own behalf. The spirit of the plant frees our will.

In addition to strengthening our willpower, the essence has become an important remedy for those with environmental sensitivity and are very sensitive to earth changes, city energy, geopathic stress, solar flares, electromagnetic frequencies (computers, phones, solar flares). It helps shed the energies that can congest in our aura and throw our body off balance. I also use the essence for clearing spaces in homes, offices, and other spaces because it helps disperse distorted energies and invoke harmony. The essence has an effect on balancing the earth's nervous system, too. You can place drops on crystals in a room, on sticks, stones placed in each direction, or sprinkle drops in a bowl of water or around the space with intention.

• "When I first started using Red Columbine it wasn't clear exactly the impact it was having on me, but recently it called me to start using it again and I kept having this vision of red-clear nectar flowing through my body as if it was flowing with all of my meridians clearing my energetic pathways," Abby shared.

• Bonnie wrote, "Red Columbine feels like it gets energy moving. It is a good essence for me to work with when I feel as if I am holding in emotions, creating a buildup of emotional energy that can make my whole being feel tense. Red Columbine assists me in releasing that pent up energy, especially by guiding me to express myself more physically—to hike, garden, dance—as a way of moving the energy out of me. It feels quite strengthening, balancing and clearing at the same time, similar to how I have felt following an acupuncture treatment."

- "I have used this essence to help me adapt to environments that feel foreign or make me feel like I want to retreat inside, close down or harden. I feel it allows me permission to take up space and to be soft and open to what I meet maintaining my integrity and truth. It also helps me clarify my intentions so that my actions align," Jill C. wrote.

Meet Red Columbine at Beacon Rock in June.

Red-flowering Currant

Ribes sanguineum
Affirmation of the Wildflower: "I am supported"
Element: Earth, Water

Acceptance • Agitation • Baby Spirits • Calming • Children • Confidence • Courage • Creativity • Detoxification • Ego • Embodiment • Exhaustion • Fear • Forgiveness • Grounding • Heart Healing • Illness • Lower-back Issues • Manifestation • Masculine/Men • Nourishing • Psychic Development • Safety • Security • Support • Stress • Trauma • Will • Worry • Chakra 1 (root), 2 (sacral), 4 (heart)

Balanced: calmly rooted in the sacrum's foundational support

Be calm, relaxed, and rooted in your foundation. Know that you are fully supported. You don't have to try so hard. From this knowing springs forth a sense of inner courage. This plant gave me a vision of a Native American woman with Red-flowering Currant in her hand. She held the red blossoms over a baby's lower back with loving care.

It is such a delight to witness pretty red flowers blooming on the Red-flowering Currant bush or small tree. They are very sweet to behold. The flower's red color signifies its medicine for the blood and our life-force energy and the root chakra which grounds our emotions. Its presence is always helpful when we are *trying too hard*. Its calming nature helps us relax and feel at peace—a perfect natural antidote to stress.

Red-flowering Currant is one of the best flower essences for quickly calming our energy, fear, and helping us feel more supported in life. The essence grounds our kidneys, where we hold fear, and instills greater courage to our heart. It's a helpful flower essence to take when we are feeling financially challenged or lack a sense of security. These concerns may relate to lower back issues. Like a base of support, this flower provides a greater sense of inner-security. Everything is going to be alright.

Over the years, this flower essence has come up repeatedly for working with baby spirits either to heal them, release them, or communicate with them. Whether it is a baby spirit getting ready for conception or birth, baby spirits that were released through pregnancy termination or other means, or a spirit of a baby that needs to move on, Red-flowering Currant helps babies and their parents (or would-be parents) find greater peace through healing and closure.

Placing drops of this essence on the palms of the hands and rubbing it into the sacrum or kidney area can help release emotional and body patterns from the root chakra.

"I'm your base of support
when you are flying too high
or off on a tangent
you can come back in touch
with me

We need touch-stones
to secure our place
in the world—a place
to come back to

I am yours—your home
away from home
Your sense of security

All-encompassing love
held deep in the sacrum
Our secure foundation for
being here

I'll be your comfort
I'll be your support
I Love you"

- When Dani first decided to take the summer off, her eye started twitching from a sense of stress regarding her decision. Red-flowering Currant helped her shift her feelings so she felt supported in her decision to work less. Her eye relaxed. The twitch was gone.

- Richard said, "I was feeling really stressed." After he used the flower essence, he said, "I felt like the pressure was taken off me."

- I could tell Doris was stressed out and needed Red-flowering Currant. "At this point, I definitely feel out there on a limb by myself and don't yet know how to find, or allow to come to me, the right resources." Doris felt like she was trying too hard to make things happen in her career and financial life.

- "I told Camilla that I was feeling isolated and lonely when I drove in my car. She placed the wildflower card [*Sacred Spirit Deck*] on my dashboard and gave me some Red-flowering Currant flower essence. The message 'I am supported' written on the card and transmitted to me through the essence changed my experience of driving. I now feel happy in my car! I also use it in my practice to help clients open to seek and receive support in their lives from Spirit, Nature, and people," Katie S. wrote.

Meet Red-flowering Currant at Ainsworth State Park - Horsetail Falls in April.

Silky Lupine

Lupinus sericeus
Affirmation of the Wildflower: "I focus my mind"
Element: Air

Ancestor Healing • Beauty • Clairvoyance • Clarity • Communication • Community • Detoxification • Fear • Focus • Goddess • Intuition • Manifestation • Meditation • Mindfulness • Mental Balance • Replenishment • Telepathy • Trauma • Chakra 6 (3rd eye)

Balanced: clearly focused and beautiful communication

Dance with the purple Goddess as she offers you mental clarity and new forms of expression and communication. Silky Lupine teaches non-verbal communication. Allow her to assist you in focusing and clearing the mind for meditation, channeling, and relating with mindfulness.

Fields of Lupine in the spring always glow with a stunning purple light that illuminates the shamanic realms and awakens our 3rd eye. Some grow in difference hues. Her spirit is very alive, joyful, giddy even. She loves to be greeted with respect and honor and a sense of reverence. I have seen her spirit dance with purple swirls of light. She is beautiful; she mirrors our beauty back to us. This wildflower adores her neighbor, the sunny yellow Balsamroot.

From the legume family, Lupine's pea-like flowers create a beautiful elegance on her erect spike. Legumes as flower essences are often used to hold communities together. Lupine loves growing in connected community. Silky Lupine's leaves are soft green with silvery hairs and fan out like a hand in palmate fashion. The plant fixes nitrogen in the soil so is adept at replenishing depleted places. Lupines were planted around Chernobyl, Ukraine after that nuclear disaster to absorb poison and detoxify the area of the effects of trauma.

The flower essence helps us open to more joy in our feminine wild energy and embodiment. Silky Lupine wants us to know we are beautiful from within. She aids in opening our intuition and spiritual sight and teaches non-verbal communication, telepathy, intuitive knowing, and multidimensional heart-mind as Oneness. She settles our mind in an uplifting way. Because she trains our mind on greater clarity, focus, and intuitive intention, she aids in our ability to be potent at manifesting.

Silky Lupine will help those that wish to expand their sense of self to encompass their inner knowing and wild beauty. When we feel limited by resistance, past trauma, fear, Lupine can help. It is perfect for intuitive development as long as we stay grounded in our expansion of the 3rd eye. Maybe that's why she loves to grow near very deeply-rooted Balsamroot.

• Abby was so excited because Silky Lupine made her feel so giddy and happy. The plant spirit was upbeat and opened her inhibitions. The tension in her jaw relaxed. "This would be a great flower essence to take and dance 5 Rhythms. It is for those that are suppressed or suffocated in some way and feel restricted, heavy, or depressed from doing that. It's a re-set button. The flower Deva says: 'You are beautiful just the way you are.'"

• Blue found the purple-blue energy of Lupine reached her higher heart and higher chakras. "The pods are thick and create a temple shape. Each pod is so prolific—fertile. She is *wild*. The wild feminine. I tried to grow Lupine and she didn't want to be *tamed* in my garden." Blue felt Lupine flower essence would be great for those that are in relationships with people that want to *keep* you the way *they* want you to be but you feel sick and wasting away from lack of true feminine wild power. The wild need their freedom.

• Heather took some drops of Silky Lupine flower essence and was instantly transported to a field of Lupine with a Goddess wearing a skirt of Lupine. They gazed into each other's eyes. She noticed the open petals and the *hook* shape of the flower and its revealing opening. The essence brought a feeling of softness in strength and gave her a sense that someone understood her. The Goddess held her hands out to Heather and gave her dance and sparkle.

Meet Silky Lupine at Tom McCall Nature Preserve in April-May.

The Columbia River

Affirmation of Water Place: "*The sacred journey of the heart begins at my source and flows into an ocean of oneness*"

Balanced: surrendering to the flow of life through care and nurturing of self and source-waters

The Columbia River is a major artery of life-sustaining water for the planet and one of the few major rivers that runs East-West. Its source waters are in British Columbia, Canada and it flows and connects with hundreds of tributaries in Washington, Idaho, Oregon including the Snake River before it reaches the ocean. Thousands of salmon make the journey from birthplace to ocean and ultimately return home. When you bless the source-waters, you're offering flows all the way to the sea.

Physically, or in spirit form, we can connect with the spirit of water, and the water elementals, at the beginning source, the place where the water first emerges and rises from the earth. This is a place to renew our sacred relationship with the earth. Visit the source waters in the spring or meditate and imagine being at the source waters—the womb waters of Mother Earth. It's an opportunity to offer gratitude to our Mother for our birth and for her life-giving water. There is great power and possibility in blessing and praying at the source. As the river flows, the collected energy frequency of our prayers, songs, and gratitude feed and energize the waters, lands, animals, and humans downstream. Our prayers gather with everyone else's prayers all the way to the sea.

Nchi'i - Wana is one of the indigenous names for the big river that serves as life-source for the people that have lived and gathered at her shores since ancient times including the Yakama, Nez Perce, Celilo Wyam, Klickitat, and Confederated Tribes of Warm Springs. We are asked to honor, respect, and protect the water, home of the sacred salmon. How the salmon and the water are cared for reflects how we care for the earth, and ourselves. We all thrive in flowing river systems. We all thrive when we care for each other.

My Native American friend, Marshall "Golden Eagle" Jack, learned the old ways from his Paiute Grandmother. As a child, he noticed many people in his tribe were gone in the spring. He asked his Grandmother, "Where did everyone go?" She told him that the tribal elders and medicine people go up to the forest for ceremony and prayers to energize the source waters for the lands. Led by the Grandmothers, they bless, pray, and care for the water and trees and animals in the mountains so that all the people, plants, animals, and lands downstream will be healthy and strong for the year.

Our purpose as humans is to nurture planets. The spirit of the big river calls us to come down to its banks and give our gratitude. This simple intentional act makes a huge impact, more than we can ever know, and actually feeds and energizes the whole river system, the lands, and all who feed or live upon it. This is something we can do. It's joyful and brings peace and flow into our lives. We receive healing when we are of service in this way.

The Columbia River essence of place returns us to our own beginning spirit, or personal emotional source waters, for renewal of our journey on this planet. It honors our origins and path, directs our flow, and teaches us how to receive and give and receive again. The essence helps us bond more deeply with our Mother through her source-waters. The spirit of Salmon asks for commitment to nurture ourselves and our planet. It calls us to flow *with* the waters of our life and then, one day, return home.

The Forest

Affirmation of Place: "I walk deeper into my heart to feel who I am"

Balanced: open to nature's wildness in seeking our magical self

The Forest is a sacred place for spiritual connection, healing, beauty, and a greater sense of your true self. Enter the Forest and breathe deeply. Allow yourself to feel at peace. Walk from your heart-center to attune to the language of nature and commune with the forest beings. Who are you now?

The Forest is a place to *be* and a place to *feel*. We are nourished by this sacred place of incredible, rich beauty made by trees, plants, flowers, wildlife, birds, rocks, fungi, waters, nature spirits and elementals. The forest is life-giving. We can feel and sense its generosity and vibrant health in its offering of fresh air, soft earth, dappled sun and warmth, cool dew, bogs, and streams that enrich the green realms. Plants of the forest are our partners in life: our in-breath of oxygen is the forest's out-breath of CO_2, our out-breath is the forest's in-breath. Trees want us to be aware of how intimately we are linked, from birth to death, with the forest through our breath. Trees are the lungs of our planet.

In the wilderness, we have an opportunity to become part of something larger. We remember who we are. I was visiting one of my favorite forests near Panther Creek with a friend. It was dusk. He encouraged us to head back before dark. I broke down crying as we walked out: "This is where I live. I want to stay." I was overcome with sadness for leaving my family and friends in the forest. The spirit of the forest knows me. The fairies, Devas, and elementals were eager to play, commune, and share their pleasures. Dusk is the fairies' *in-between* time. Their activity flourishes in these darkening hours. Forest community is magical and emboldens our sense of adventure as it transforms our very nature. Fairy Tales take us into The Forest to meet life, face death, and access our own gifts, strength, and creative capacity. Can we make it out of the forest alive? Who will we be when we emerge from the forest?

Every forest is unique. Trees, terrain, rainfall and sun create very different places. In the Columbia River Gorge, we have temperate rainforests in the west with Big-leaf Maple, Fir, Western Hemlock, Western Redcedar. In Hood River to The Dalles, Pine-Oak Woodlands and Cottonwood dominate. Desert grasslands with Ponderosa Pine and Lodgepole Pine grow further east. The most magnificent forests are home to old growth trees—our ancient ancestors. Every forest carries it own special medicine. I've experienced that in Saguaro cactus forests, Joshua Tree forests, Redwood forests, Bristlecone Pine forests, old growth Sitka Spruce forests, Hawaiian rainforests, and Adirondack forests. In Japan, doctors prescribe *shinrin-yoku (*forest bathing) for their patients as a form of stress management to relax and live more healthy lives. Forest bathing is simply taking a walk in the woods.

The Forest essence of place gives us a space to find and feel our own deep nature. Breathe as One with nature. We receive grounding back into the earth that sets everything back into right relationship and harmony. It reminds us to visit The Forest to find what we seek. It is here that we open up to the mysteries of life and death as we venture further on our quest.

Tiger Lily
Lilium columbianum
Affirmation of the Wildflower: "*Creating is my power*"
Element: Water, Fire

Anger • Balance • Children • Compassion • Courage • Creativity • Dignity • Empowerment • Feminine/Women • Food Issues • Grounding • Manifestation • Menopause • Receptivity • Relationships • Self-esteem • Self-image • Self-worth • Sexuality • Shame • Trust • Vulnerability • Will • Chakra 1 (root), 2 (sacral), 5 (throat)

Balanced: untamed feminine creative-sexual power

The energy of a wild tiger merges with a gentle feminine lily to unleash the power of creation. Tap into your potent capacity for infinite expression. Fuel your life-force with wild abandon. This wildflower wants to be heard. "Create!" Tiger Lily shouts!

Tiger Lily is strongly colored for a lily—bright fiery orange with dark brown spots. Tiger Lily is like a cross between a gentle lily and a wild animal, a Tigress! Water (lilies) and Fire (orange) make steam! Maybe we need this *wild* beauty to fund our creativity? Our sexuality? Our world?

Tiger Lily nourishes and directs the expression of our wild, creative feminine. She can be an important ally for women in peri-menopause or menopause. What the world needs most right now is our grounded creativity embodied and expressed from the feminine creative power source. Being orange colored *and* a lily heightens its effects on the feminine emotional and creative power center, our 2nd chakra. It can also bring fresh, pulsing energy to awaken women's wombs, fallopian tubes, ovaries, and yonis.

Tigers can represent fear, too. Its strong brown spots remind us of our resistance to power, shadows, and the need for Mother Earth's rooting. Its flower is directed towards the Earth, grounding our wild creative impulses into the earth through our feeling chakra, the sacral or 2nd chakra. Its splayed back petals show an amazing openness and willingness to be expressive and vulnerable to our deepest core instincts.

In 2005, Tiger Lily said… "It is time for women to embrace their creative power! Create! Create! Women have been enablers. Create! Create!"

In 2010, Tiger Lily said it was a hugely important flower … "CREATE THE LIFE YOU WANT. YOU HAVE THE POWER TO DO THIS!"

The spirit of the Tiger Lily said it is a *power tamer*, helping to consolidate raw energy into useable power—creative, sexual life-force energy. We need to step into our creative birthright instead of allowing co-dependent or submissive patterns to get in the way. For example, this essence is helpful for creating clearer sexual energy boundaries between partners. Tiger Lily strengthens the 2nd chakra and releases the need to be an enabler or martyr—giving our creative power and energy away to others or side-stepping power instead of claiming and owning it ourselves. The Tigress will add power to our own dreams and a balance of the yin and yang polarities.

When I was doing daily physical Hanna Somatic work to open a tight sacrum, Tiger Lily was a potent ally. I felt her pulsing energy in my pelvis very gently awakening the fire of my creative-sexual-feeling power. As I stretched my hips deeply, I yawned as the sleeping energy was stirred awake. I found awakening this power a delicate process. I wanted to honor my fear (Tiger) yet move beyond it. I saw how Tiger Lily created links between my left and right hips, balancing inner polarities, and integrating masculine and feminine in my body. The energy moved like a figure eight between my right and left pelvis.

• During a flower essence class, RaVen had a strong experience after taking and meditating with Tiger Lily. A very powerful sensation came to her 2nd chakra about her power to manifest. Also, she saw a vision of an orange tabby cat, named Tiger Lily, that she had a special bond with in Hawaii. She had a vision of the cat coming out of her heart chakra during the meditation.

• After a meditation that circulated energy into Quoia's 2nd chakra, she felt her sexual energy awakening after a long winter. This opening invited comment from the person next to her, *"OOOh! A Tigress!"* This experience drew her to take the Tiger Lily flower essence over time to open herself to her creative-sexual source energy.

Meet Tiger Lily at Multnomah Falls in June and Larch Mountain Corridor in July.

Trillium
Trillium ovatum
Affirmation of the Wildflower: "I rebirth my feminine"
Element: Water

Aura Repair • Boundaries • Birth • Compassion • Courage • Creativity • Embodiment • Empowerment • Feminine/Women • Food Issues • Happiness • Heart Healing • Intuition • Midwifery • Mothering Issues • Pregnancy • Purification • Purpose • Rebirth • Receptivity • Relationships • Rites of Passage • Self-esteem • Self-expression • Self-worth • Sensitivity • Sexuality • Shame • Stress • Support • Surrender • Trust • Chakra 2 (sacral), 4 (heart), 6 (3rd eye)

Balanced: Earth-honoring Goddess, or inner-Goddess, empowered in compassion, love, and life purpose
Trillium is the midwife's flower to support and assist all forms of birthing or re-birthing because, when the process begins there is no going back. The wildflowers' purity, compassion, and strength of purpose are empowering. The healing signature of three petals and three leaves represents the power of Creation.

Called Birthroot or Wake-robin by midwives, the Trillium bulb was used as medicine to assist with pregnancy and the birthing process. Today, homeopathic Trillium is used in childbirth and to assist in processing grief. It is telling that Trillium's Latin name is *ovatum*. Ovary energy is the seat of women's potent, fertile creative fire energy. To be on a creative path, we need to reclaim and *own* the energy of our ovaries to build and feed our creative fire. Trillium flower essence can bring awareness to how we can claim personal creative space to do that.

Trilliums are magical flowers that grow in the shade of trees of Oregon and Washington. They bloom pure white in the spring during nature's time of rebirth, and then turn pink, the color of healing and Universal Love energies, after pollination. The petals and leaves always grow in multiples of three, a lily signature. Trillium's shape focuses a vortex of energy down into the Earth.

Initially, I was very resistant in getting to know the Trillium Devas as they held the seeds to my life purpose. The white lilies hold feminine wisdom and creative power. I was not ready to see my immense creative power nor was I entirely comfortable with my full spiritual inheritance as a *midwife for the soul*. Trillium reminded me of past lives where I was persecuted as an herbalist and midwife. When I allowed myself to move beyond karma and receive its medicine, Trillium brought potent healing to my re-birthing process.

More recently, in a shamanic journey, Trillium showed up to assist me in a spiritual initiation with the 13 Grandmothers of Creation. Trillium represents the trinity: three stages of a woman's life—maiden, mother, and crone aspects. The Trillium brought healing to my feminine heart and activated my work with Earth Mother.

As stronger cycles of the divine feminine emerge, Trillium helps us birth into new cycles of golden consciousness.

> *"The white lilies help us break through old structures created by humans to serve the old Gods—or beliefs. They create doorways to spiritual and angelic forces. Energy transferred for womankind. The lilies say: "No need to understand us as much as open to our energies and allow us to love you."*

The flower essence helps in the healing of women's cycles, fertility, sacred sexuality, and emotional cleansing. Trillium and other white lilies can help clear sexual abuse, grief, and reproductive trauma as well as purify the body with angelic light, love, and compassion. Lilies bring celebration and joy and give women permission to be women. Trillium aligns us with the birthing and spiritual rebirthing process.

• Sara used Trillium to integrate and re-align after a very deep healing shift within her root chakra during a sacred sexuality workshop.

• During a flower essence class, Katie took the flower essence and experienced a profound healing and directive energy from the Trillium Deva. The Deva told her to shift her job from her nursing work in intensive care to the labor and delivery area of the hospital. She was feeling extremely stressed in her work. "Trillium got the process started for me, and I knew that I could no longer work as much as I was. So, I've cut my schedule back by 75%! And I'm concentrating on studying Chinese medicine."

Katie shared more after taking the essence for a few weeks. "Trillium is a mover. Once the birthing process starts we can't turn back. We can only move forward once we receive the gift of knowing what we need to do in order for more love and freedom to come forth."

Katie sat with the blooming Trillium flowers. "The message I got from Trillium was, 'The Earth has been rejoicing since you've arrived!' She has been rejoicing that we are all here doing this Great Work of transformation and healing. We are birthing the higher vibrations of our light bodies into the planet and this human form. We are naturally opening to Nature! There is great courage with Trillium. Courage to look, to feel, and to act."

Meet Trillium in the forests near Bridal Veil Falls in April.

Wahclella Falls

Affirmation of Water Place: "*I birth myself anew in the presence of the nature spirits*"

Balanced: magical sense of the interconnectedness with all living things in nature

This trail invites you on a journey into the magical, ancestral, and elemental realms of nature. Walk with the spirit of the wildflowers, Western Redcedar, waterfalls, a singing river, and massive moss-covered stone beings. The fairies, Devas, gnomes, and water spirits alight around the sacred caves of Mother Earth's body. Wahclella Falls is a Temple of Nature for the waters of your heart.

Every time I journey to the falls, I transform. It is the nature of a sacred place, it changes us. I know this place reaches the deepest longings of my soul and nurtures my heart. One day, I was able to pause and witness a huge heart expansion when I brought a dear friend. As we walked, I was suddenly overcome with loving feelings for him and felt my heart expand wide in my chest. I observed that my heart chakra was glowing and spinning like a wheel of beautiful colors of red, gold, and white—new colors for my heart chakra. When I looked over at him, his heart chakra was glowing in the same manner as mine.

Merging with the magic of Wahclella Falls is medicine for the heart. Tree guardians greet us. There is a transition onto a forest trail by the first magical waterfall called Munra Falls and watchful rock and tree spirits. A small bridge allows us to stand and receive the sound of the waterfall Deva in her whispery tones of spray. She told me she will grant us wishes and give us messages and offer healing. Try toning with her. The trail flows by the edge of Tanner Creek into a basalt canyon with massive mossy rocks in the river and walls of basalt rising on either side. There are numerous ancient trees, plants, ferns, flowers, and moss growing along the trail that wish to engage with us as we walk. They embrace us with very tender, gentle energy if we walk slowly and mindfully. This place anchors us with the quality of *endurance*.

Every few steps is another habitat for fairies, gnomes, mermaids, Devas, spirits of plants, and tree guardians. And, ultimately we arrive at her temple space of caves, a sweet waterfall merging into a thunderous waterfall that flows into a huge rounded rock splash pool, giant Western Redcedar trees, and spray-soaked misty viewpoints. All noise is cancelled out due to the thunder of the water. In this Temple of Nature, the waterfall is singing hymns and preaching the Truth for those with ears to hear.

Wahclella Falls essence of place helps us re-connect with source energy, earth energy, the magic of nature spirits in the sacredness of nature. Our listening practice deepens. It reminds us to feed our hearts with nature's spiritual nourishment and let ourselves merge with its beauty and power and delight. This place strengthens our *endurance*—our ability to keep going when facing adversity. Mother Earth takes care of her children here, and we are her children, too.

Western Redcedar
Thuja plicata
Affirmation of the Tree: "I am a Tree of Life"
Element: Water, Earth

Agitation • Ancestor Healing • Centering • Clearing • Conduit of Light • Connection • Divine Connection • Grounding • Healing • Purifying • Strength • Tree of Life • Water Spirit Connection • Wisdom • Worry • Chakra (all)

Balanced: standing in our *wisdom body* like a Tree of Life grounded in the earth and connected to the heavens

The Tree of Life for the Pacific Northwest is honored for its food, medicine, shelter, transportation, and endless giving. Its wisdom is deep and ancient. Now, it is time to activate your energy like the Tree of Life—to become a conduit between heaven and earth as well. Your connection to earth and the heavens grants you full access to the wisdom body of your ancestors and the ancient ones. When burned ceremonially, Cedar is purifying and healing.

I developed a deep love of our native Western Redcedar tree at Panther Creek Falls as I sat on her roots by the creek and melted into her body. I began hearing messages from the ancient one. Grandmother told me about my *wisdom body*, a part of my knowing that is linked with the wisdom of the whole earth body. She encourages everyone to tap into their own knowing, be a conduit of light, and become a Tree of Life that connects heaven with earth like a tree. I felt very humbled and grateful to hear her gentle teachings.

More recently, I co-lead a Western Redcedar Medicine Circle with Saliha Abrams and Katie Silva. Before the event we gathered in a circle among six beautiful ancient Cedars. As we attuned to the energy of the trees I saw my blood turn green as if the plant realms were pulling me back to the green realms. Then a bubble of blue formed around my aura and blue blood flowed in my etheric veins showing my celestial connection. It resonated with the way the tree roots grounds us into the earth (green) and connects us into the stars (blue) with its high branches. My *wisdom body* is now circulating with red, green, and blue blood through my veins and synchronizing my blood circulation in my multidimensional body.

A song came through Katie as we sat in communion with the tree. It feels like a lullaby. When we sing it, I feel the medicine of the tree become deeply anchored within my being.

"I am the one who comes to you in your dreams
I am the Grandmother who's mouth is a river of life
Drink deeply my child, Drink deeply my child, Drink deeply my child, Drink deeply my child, Drink deeply from the river of life
Dream deeply my child, Dream deeply my child, Dream deeply my child, Dream deeply my child, Dream deeply with the river of life"

The tree essence of Western Redcedar brings a beautiful blending of the elementals of water and earth to help us ground and keep our energy flowing simultaneously. The essence can help us visualize, sense, or feel how to ground through our first chakra (root) to cleanse emotions, through our feet to connect to earth's healing energy, and through aligning with our *wisdom body* (3rd eye and aura) grounded through our central channel. A grounding practice is a way to stay healthy, balanced, clear, and connected to spiritual guidance and earth energy. It is crucial to maintaining health and harmony.

Through its branches and the crown of the tree, Western Redcedar helps us connect with divine spirit above—source energy. She helps keep our conduit of energy, the light-filled *central channel* of our body around the spine, clear and light-filled for better connection with source. She lulls us back to the present moment. The tree essence soothes agitation and worry. It can help release what is not serving us and enliven our relationship with nature.

• Heather felt such gratitude for the relationships she was forming with trees as she learned to connect with their spirit and medicine. To her, Western Redcedar offered caresses and hugs and the immediate felt-sense of her roots connecting down into the earth and grounding her in all ways.

• Kim shared her experiences with Western Redcedar. "The needle of my inner compass has been spinning wildly lately, taking the magnetic pull of my own heart's need for belonging sometimes to the brink of my sanity. I'm working out some karmic forces that put me on these divergent paths, I now know from talking with Western Redcedar. The image of a compass and Western Redcedar are intertwined, almost like a holographic image; seeing one thing from this angle, another from that angle, whenever I smell it."

"Is it possible that the plant Devas have been directing my life all along, drawing my map? You used the phrase *re-homing oneself* when you did my [flower essence] reading. One person says my return here is hurting me. Another says I MUST stay put. So I want to accept the discomfort I'm experiencing now and heal this heart so I can get on with my work."

"For me, the thing that is most profound is how STRONG and POWERFUL the forces of the plants are. Just when I think nothing is happening, just when I throw some shade (no pun intended!) on the whole plant spirit-as-true-medicine idea, plant spirit moves mountains for me. Plant spirit shows me, look, I'm bringing you to forests and deserts and canyons to show you where your life is. Trust it."

• Katie S. wrote, "Western Redcedar essence connects me with the deep watery well of my own being and the waters of the earth. It aligns me with grace between heaven and earth and rocks me in a sacred canoe of support and relieves me of my burdens. It teaches me about the balance between masculine and feminine energies and earth and sky. It teaches me where to put my focus and attention—on those aspects that are most heart-felt and meaningful. It opens the door to deeper wisdom in life situations and an eagle-eye view of life."

• Jill C. shared her experience. "The day we created the essence I remember it was the first time I truly felt a deep connection to the Cedar tree. I remember it was like meeting my grandmother and touching a generational connection much deeper than my family roots. I remember feeling a deep sense of being held and connected to such a soft, deep, and luminous love energy. I felt as it her arms were around my body in a spacious yet penetrating way allowing me to feel safe. This is when I connected to the feminine earth sense of grounding rather than the more familiar masculine sense of strength."

"When I use the essence for myself and for my clients I use it to find that calm, grounded strength and support. I find that it helps me find that inner stillness and trust in a chaotic and changing world. I can feel her roots anchoring me and her trunk holding me up and her branches like arms of an embrace. I also feel that it reminds me of my deep wisdom that is passed on to me through the ancients. It allows me to remember that I may not know in my head but I do in my heart."

Meet Western Redcedar at Panther Creek Waterfall.

Western Rhododendron
Rhododendron macrophyllum
Affirmation of the Wildflower: "I enhance my experience of compassion"
Element: Air

Acceptance • Attachment • Authentic Relating • Beauty • Circles • Councils • Community • Compassion • Empathy • Heart Healing • Identity • Nourishment • Nurturing • Relationships • Self-love • Support • Unconditional Love • Chakra 4 (heart), 3 (solar plexus)

Balanced: A compassionate and loving heart in beautiful authentic relationships

A delightful surprise awaits you when you enter the dark forest where the wild Rhododendron flowers bloom. A shock of huge, pink, luscious blossoms color the woods with beauty and love. Dance in a circle around them—a dance of love and compassion for yourself.

Deep in the mountain forests of Oregon, native Western Rhododendron flowers blossom with delight. Big showy blossoms create circles of energy around the plants larger body. Their buds, flowers, leaves lay open to receive divine love. When I was making the flower essence, I was guided to walk in a circle around the large bush and sing the following song:
The Circle of Life, The Circle of Life, The Circle of Life, May you Follow
The Circle of Life, The Circle of Life, The Circle of Life, May you Lead
The Western Rhododendron song amplifies the energy of circling. Circling is the ancient form of community when we sit in Council. Circles level out relationships and bring everyone to equal standing. Sometimes we are leaders and sometimes followers. Our way of relating is very fluid. Circles enhance community and heal our hearts. Studies have proven that those who enjoy circles of support make faster and stronger recovery from illness or loss. Everything in nature is a circle—cycles, seasons, patterns, shapes, flows of energy. Orbs are circular. Circles are feminine in nature.

Compassion holds the circle. This flower essence teaches us about healthy compassion as a state of grace. When our empathy is balanced, we can be centered in compassion—we can feel care and concern for others from a neutral space of love. We honor everyone's experience and struggle and adopt a state of acceptance where we judge nothing and allow others to have their own experience without interference. We know that is how we, and others, grow to know God.

Western Rhododendron can help when we *over-identify* with another's struggles and get pulled into an unhealthy energy pattern—the never-ending triad of being either a rescuer-healer-perpetrator. These attachments to outcome result when we are not in right alignment—we stepped out of the circle. Western Rhododendron helps us heal our own heart wounding so we can be cleaner in our compassion.

The flower essence steps forward when we are learning compassion and how to hold ourselves in ways that make our heart stronger. Native American elders say: "Do what makes your heart the strongest." Following what is beautiful makes our heart strong. Western Rhododendron leads us to the beauty of their glorious pink blossoms that can heal our hearts and envelope us in their compassionate presence. It helps us make connection to circles that feed and nourish us spiritually and provide healthy authentic relating. And it helps us learn to be in Council with all beings of nature.

• Jill C. shared, "I have used this essence to soften into grief and keeping my heart open during vulnerable times. I feel like it creates a sense of soft support and love around my emotions and my pain. It is like an angel is holding my heart steady and sweetly so that I can relax and trust. When I worked with the plant itself, the mantra "Om Mani Padme Hum" came into my heart. The jewel is in the lotus. The wisdom is in the heart. I know that an open heart allows the wisdom to pour in and out."

Meet Western Rhododendron in Lost Lake Forests in June

White Salmon River

Affirmation of Water Place: "I remember! I am wild and free"

Balanced: the flowing, bubbling, effervescent enthusiasm of self-sovereignty

One of the biggest dam-release projects in history restored the lower section of the river after almost 100 years. The salmon quickly returned. The White Salmon River reminds you that full sovereignty belongs to every being: a river, a mermaid, ferns, salmon, and yourself.

It is powerful to be on the wild river and feel the raw elemental power of its wild river spirit, mermaids and mermen, and water elementals and undines. Rafting down the White Salmon River with Heather Kowalewski and a Mermaid Whitewater Rafting trip we co-lead, we pulled our raft out near the former site of the dam. I could feel the trauma in the rocks and stagnation of the land. We brought crystals and flowers and gave prayers for the river and offered our love and gratitude. We sang and prayed for the restoration of nature at this place. We felt the energy lighten, and I could sense new nature spirits returning. The next time we visited the site, there were more nature spirits, the land welcomed us, I saw etheric rainbows, and we sensed evidence of healing including a frog watching from its hole like a guardian spirit.

In 2011, I was back in Hood River with my partner for a few days when someone told us the dam on the White Salmon River, a tributary of the Columbia River, was coming down. I got chills up and down my body! I had seen visions and done water ceremony for the rivers. Now it was time to witness a new era—freedom for the waters. Marshall "Golden Eagle" Jack, Ellie Trichter, Robbee Lapp, and I perched high on the cliffs above the mouth of the White Salmon River where it meets the Columbia River and prayed and watched the water flow change. It was a transformative moment.

In the years since, new land has formed, plants and wildflowers bloom, and the wild flow of water is carving out new places for plants, wildlife, and beauty to take hold once again on its way into the Columbia River. There is a buzz of energy around the river from all the people who love it so much and depend on the river for their *lovelihood* (my version of livelihood).

White Salmon River essence of place helps us break through what holds us back so we can remember how to run free and wild, bubbling, whirling, flowing, churning, effervescent, enthusiastic, remembering, surrendering, and ultimately knowing how to return home. We can choose freedom and self-sovereignty (self-rule). The river teaches us respect and honoring of the power within water and self-respect and self-honoring of our own inner-waters—our emotional and feeling nature.

photo: Heather Kowalewski, AllAdventuresRafting.com

Wild Rose
Rosa pisocarpa
Affirmation of the Wildflower: "I am passionate about life"
Element: Earth

Anger • Apathy • Birth Trauma • Heart Healing • Fairy-Nature Connection • Grief • Inner-child • Intimacy • Loss • Nervous System • Passion • Relationship • Self-love • Unconditional Love • Chakra 1 (root), 4 (heart), 6 (3rd eye), 7 (crown)

Balanced: renewed passion and love of our humanity

This gentle pink healer can help you open to more joy. Wild rose renews a tender heart and helps you repair, restore, and re-balance your nervous system. Let the sweet smell of Wild Rose activate your blossoming process.

The light pink Wild Rose grows near my home and for the healing and support of humans everywhere. It's signature of five petals refers to its medicine for the five-fingered ones—humanity. Its sweet nature renews our love of life and delights our inner-child. Our children instinctively know this is good and beautiful medicine. There are thorns on the Wild Roses, too. Life can hurt, but we will bloom again with patience and unconditional love. Wild Rose loves to assist us.

Rose is a wonderful healer for the heart. I've made a rose flower essence from the dark fuchsia pink rose—a passionate beauty—but this light pink rose heals in a more tender, gentle, sweet way. Pink is the color of universal healing and unconditional love. Many of us need to care for our hearts, and our inner-child, with tenderness, kindness, and love. Rose gives us permission to do that.

The flower essence has the power to reach back in time to help us heal birth trauma. We often play out our lives based on how we come into this world, so this process gives us a chance to change the way we walk in this world. All roses support the alignment and repair of our electrical system (nervous system). This keeps our energy system flowing un-interrupted. Rose flower essences are wonderful companions for anchoring cranial sacral therapy adjustments.

Wild Rose is so generous in holding our heart and offering unlimited love vibrations. If we feel we missed out on receiving the love we wanted, it's never too late to welcome in the frequencies we need to feel loved and enthusiastic about life. Let rose hug you close.

The spirit of Wild Rose says, "Shore up your cup of love and let it pour out in all directions because you are so full."

- On taking the Wild Rose flower essence, Hannah had a dream she was going to meet someone. She met a man shortly after and for the first time in two years felt romantic interest. She told me she was so happy because the flower essence got her back into her ritual practice—she was so excited to build a new altar with plants, sacred objects, and a picture of Lakshmi. She said, "I have definitely shifted. I feel an all-over opening and brought in some interesting things including the welcome commitment to my prayer practice." Hannah confided that she was debating going on pharmaceutical medication for depression. "The Wild Rose essence was very powerful. It really helped. I didn't realize how heartbroken I was. Now, I am drawn to the scent of roses which I never wanted to smell before. I just ordered rose essential oil. I want to get some rose-colored paint for my room. Thank you for the medicine!"

- "Sweet and appreciative." Abby saw the Wild Rose like a little jewel inside of her heart nurturing her with love and sparking gratitude for all the little precious things. "I love the Wild Rose and Buttercup flower essences together!!"

- "Wild Rose has been a lovely companion in my flower essence blend. It has truly expanded my awareness to open my heart space physically, emotionally, mentally. Its soft love has gently guided me to progress in difficult and dark areas of physical and spiritual body with comfort. After receiving Wild Rose in my essence blend, it soon appeared in other places for me reassuring me it is one of my allies. Its softness and Truth has given me confidence to manifest my deepest desires. Thank you." Brittany wrote.

Meet Wild Rose at St Cloud Wayside in May.

Willow

Salix lucida sp.
Affirmation of the Tree: *"I flow with forgiveness"*
Element: *Water*

Balance • Change • Children • Clairsentience • Detoxification • Ego • Emotional • Equilibrium • Exercise • Flexibility • Flow • Fluidity • Forgiveness • Intuition • Irritation • Judgment • Movement • Patience • Protection • Rebirth • Receptivity • Resentment • Rites of Passage • Safety • Self-doubt • Self-image • Self-pity • Support • Transformation • Trauma • Trust • Vulnerability • Will • Chakra 1 (root), 3 (solar plexus), 4 (heart)

Balanced: flexible and flowing energy and body grounded in watery nature

The flexible, fluid, and forgiving nature of Willow weaves beautiful, purposeful baskets to carry treasures of the earth. Native American Grandmothers sing The Willow Song and ask what kind of basket the particular tree or branch wants to become. The Spirit of Willow tells them.

Willows are water lovers that gather together at the water's edge and enjoy flow and movement. The trees stabilize and maintain the banks of rivers. Willow branches are flexible enough to make circles for beautiful dream catchers, weave baskets, and build sacred sweat lodges. It creates the hoop of life and represents spiritual healing and rebirth. It is known for its natural *aspirin* and pain relieving qualities. There are numerous kinds of Willow and all share fuzzy male and female flowers called catkins that bloom early in the spring.

I met an ancient Willow tree at a wetland in Washington with the biggest plant spirit I'd ever seen. The Deva was a massive, golden light that filled the whole area. It knew I wanted to connect with it, and the Deva made itself known. I connected through knowing and clairsentience—paying attention to my feelings. Its energy was very watery. I felt a *wash* of energy as if the tree was offering healing for my heart. When I thanked the tree, the wave of energy became stronger and overwhelmingly beautiful. Tears came to my eyes. The massive Willow was so grateful to receive my gratitude. Its spirit was fed by my appreciation.

The beauty of the Willow is in its flexibility, fluidity, and ability to bend and flow so easily and gracefully. The flower essence helps us move and flow and opens us to these qualities within our minds and bodies—new ways of thinking and more ease of movement. Any fixed ideas, resentments, lack of forgiveness, bitterness, or unhealthy behaviors can be gently unwound with the love of this tree. Stubbornly held attitudes can relax and shift.

People are called willowy when they are tall, thin, and graceful in movements like the tree. The flower essence flows more grace and movement into our life and is an excellent remedy to use when practicing yoga as it opens flexibility.

Weeping Willow trees look as if their hanging branches and leaves are crying. They create a private space underneath to join them and shed our tears. Willow can show us how to release pain, sadness, and other deep-seated emotions through expression of our feelings. Its watery energy moves stagnant Qi or blocked energy in the body, mind, and spirit. Willow calls us to circle back to our birth and receive healing through *rebirth*.

In a shamanic journey with the Willow flower essence I was immediately merged with the spirit of water… flowing downstream on a nest of Willow twigs with joy and freedom. I experienced delight. Then I flew up in the air and noticed I was covered with long branches of Willow leaves for arms and legs. "Oh, how beautiful! I am *Willow Woman*." My hands formed circular mudras in the sky—round, a circle, a ring, the Sun. A gold ring came out of my mouth. I picked it up and gave it back to the Sun. The Sun received it. After this journey, I found golden-colored Willow branches and wove a larger golden ring and placed it on my water altar. I realized that Willow was showing me something about marriage. The marriage of all the elements within my body—Air, Fire, Water, Earth—created Ethers and *Willow Woman*.

• Monica writes, "I had been working on accepting my duties and callings. In the process, I found myself fighting against my intuition. In the flower essence class, I decided to make a formula to address my inflexibility. Immediately, the bottle of Willow essence "jumped" out at me. After taking a few drops, I sensed energy moving to my arms and legs. Within two minutes, a wave of energy started working on my very stiff lower back. The stiffness was a physical manifestation of holding back mentally. I was so amazed that the Willow essence knew what to do with me right away. Needless to say, I also use it for physical flexibility!

• Taking Willow, Loralai felt her energy flowing much more in her body. She felt more physically flexible so she stretched and exercised her body more often because she really wanted to and it felt good. It also drew her attention to places in her life where she wasn't flowing, and it gave her more will to do something to make a change.

• Nance had her childhood love of Willow surface as she took the essence during cancer therapy. She said it was a comforting and safe shelter during the storm. The Weeping Willow tree offered her inner-child a place she could crawl into to feel safe—an escape place—where she could be rocked by the tree or weep with the movement of the willow branches.

• After taking Willow flower essence, Inez was taken to meet an ancient Willow tree. The tree was wise and strong, yet it cared for her tenderly. She saw a garden. The altar of flowers and crystals reflected aspects of her inner-self. Suddenly, she was pulled through a dark crevice towards a red light. She had a rebirthing. She felt and experienced what her birth felt like— being pulled through, in shock, and then feeling very young, very needy, and vulnerable. Inez shared, "I was cared for and placed under a Willow tree and all my spirit allies surrounded me."

• Abby shared her experience of taking the Willow flower essence. "I immediately saw myself under water in a deep, calm ocean. It was the feeling of having your whole body held by the water and it felt so good. No gravity. Peaceful and calm. It made me crave being submerged in water so badly. It reminded me of when I was little, we had one of those 3-foot above ground pools. I would swim around in a circle and it felt so good to be under water with it flowing over me. Every time I circled, I would say 'one more time 'round,' over and over. It was always hard to get out. Afterwards, it made me crave water all day. Even at this moment, I want to go swimming."

Meet Willow on Indian Creek Trail in Hood River.

Yarrow
Achillea millefolium
Affirmation of the Wildflower: "I am pure & strong"
Element: Air

Anger • Aura Repair • Boundaries • Children • Clairvoyance • Death/Dying • Detoxification • Dream Consciousness • Embodiment • Fatigue • Immunity • Inner-strength • Menopause • Nightmares • Purification • Protection • Self-assertiveness • Sensitivity • Stress • Surrender • Transformation • Vulnerability • Chakra 4 (heart), 5 (solar plexus), 7 (crown)

Balanced: healed and energetically protected with strong purifying light

Yarrow weaves a protective shield of white light within your aura to enhance your life-force energy, boundaries, and immunity. The plant can assist healers and those who like to help and nurture others. You can tell the plant is Yarrow by its feathery leaves and bitter scent.

Yarrow is a hardy healing ally with widespread growth throughout the Pacific Northwest. Its vibrant collections of tiny white flower clusters creates an umbrella of love as it emits a potent bitter scent; its leaves look like soft plant feathers. It can grow anywhere but especially loves dry areas. I experience the spirit of Yarrow as an overseer angel protecting me with *Christ Consciousness* energy—unconditional love. It helps me enlighten my inner-essence so I can feel the strength of my divinity all around me. In *Wildflowers: Their Occult Gifts*, Hilarion channels that Yarrow releases our dreaming consciousness from lower astral regions where nightmares come from.

The flower is named for Achilles. In the legend, Achilles' mother makes a bath with Yarrow and dips her baby Achilles into the bath, holding him only by his heels. The Yarrow bath strengthened every part of the body except where she held him by his heels. The *Achilles heel* is considered the most vulnerable part of a human being. Everyone has a vulnerable place; an archetypal wounding we came here to heal. Yarrow can help us bring vulnerabilities to the surface to heal. Yarrow also has an affinity for healing the heart of healers and our core wounds. As a flower essence, it's considered *the healer's remedy*.

Yarrow's ancient name was Woundwort and Herb of Protection. The plant was important during ancient times because of its wound healing properties especially during battle. The plant was applied directly to wounds to stop the bleeding, protect it from infection, and to bring healing to the area. The plant's spirit helped heal the warriors' wounds of the heart.

Energetically, the Yarrow flower essence heals and teaches us about our aura—the protective energy field that surrounds our body—by strengthening it and creating stronger energy boundaries. Having a strong and intact aura increases our available life-force energy and creates a strong protective quality that translates to stronger physical health, emotional immunity, and energetic boundaries. Yarrow also promotes the natural healthy cleansing and detoxifying actions of ridding EMFs and radiation from the body. It is strengthening especially for those who are highly sensitive to other people's emotions and environmental influences. It is an excellent flower essence for children.

• Three-year old Colton's mother gave him Yarrow flower essence when he seemed to be acting out in ways that suggested he was off balance. After taking the Yarrow, he was stronger and more able to maintain balance.

• After an operation to repair a torn Achilles heel, Randy tested for the essence of Yarrow. His vulnerabilities were being acutely tested as he lay in the hospital room. He took the remedy and could feel an immediate sensation of being energetically aligned. Yarrow assisted his recovery process on the emotional and physical realms.

• When she sits with Yarrow or uses the flower essence, RaVen sees an image of large red haired Vikings and a shield of protection.

• Bonnie wrote: "The Yarrow and Red Columbine combo feel like a strong fortifying combo, like what I imagine receiving a blood transfusion might be like if you were in urgent need of one."

• Heather shared that after taking Yarrow flower essence she had the sensation of her head blossomed open and then the plant grounded her. It helped her feel more open. "I asked for help with my boundaries and I sensed that the plant was creating a structure that was firm around me. It helped me feel more solid. I felt release and then a softer feeling of clearing."

• Ellie O. felt a sense of boundary in her aura upon taking Yarrow flower essence. She felt armored, not like a warrior, but in a softer sense of being protected. She felt very grounded, like her feet were sinking into the ground. Her mind quieted, and she felt like she had complete control over making her own decisions. "Making decisions is the hardest thing for me," Ellie admitted.

Meet Yarrow at Horsethief Butte in June.

Affirmations of Wildflowers & Places

Flower/Place   Latin Name   Affirmation

Angelica *Angelica genuflexa* I am an Earth Angel

Ball-head Waterleaf *Hydrophyllum capitatum var. thompsonii* I open to the flow of life

Balsamroot *Balsamorhiza sagittata* I grow into my full potential

Barrett's Penstemon *Penstemon barrettiae* I know I can fly

Beacon Rock I honor the sacred lands and walk with The Ancestors

Bleeding Heart *Dicentra formosa* I cleanse my heart with love

Buttercup *Ranunculus reconditus* It's time to play!

California Poppy *Eschscholzia californica* I love myself; I value myself

Camas *Camassia quamash* I am open to everything, attached to nothing

Catherine Creek Arch I am a bridge to the cosmos

Desert Sage *Artemisia tridentata* I hold sacred space

Fairy Slipper Orchid *Calypso bulbosa* I open to new adventures

Foxglove *Digitalis purpurea* Emotional vulnerability is a gift

Green Bog Orchid *Platanthera aquilonis* I align with the heart of Mother Earth

Heart-leaf Buckwheat *Eriogonum compositum var. compositum* I am comfortable with change

Larkspur *Delphinium nuttallianum* I delight in my true voice

Mock Orange *Philadelphus lewisii* I am one-of-a-kind

Moss Nature hugs me with her love

Mt Hood (Wy'east) I ground and align with the crystalline grid of the mountain

Mt Hood Lily *Lillium Cascadia* I claim my divine beauty and space

Mullein *Verbascum thapsus* I am still in order to listen

Multnomah Falls I am the pure and precious essence of love

Ocean Spray *Holodiscus discolor* I flow with grace

Oregon Grape *Berberis aquifolium* I trust in myself

Oregon Oak *Quercus garryanna* I am strong in purpose & joy
Phantom Orchid *Eburophyton austiniae* I remove all blocks & interference
Poet's Shooting Star *Dodecatheon poeticum* I am fully present
Ponderosa Pine *Pinus ponderosa* I trust all is well
Pungent Desert Parsley *Lomatium grayii* I awaken to my true self
Queen Bead Lily *Clintonia uniflora* I am a Queen of the Light
Red Columbine *Aquilegia formosa* I free my will
Red-flowering Currant *Ribes sanguineum* I am supported
Silky Lupine *Lupinus sericeus* I focus my mind
The Columbia River The sacred journey of the heart begins at my source and flows into an ocean of oneness
The Forest I walk deeper into my heart to feel who I am
Tiger Lily *Lilium columbianum* Creating is my power
Trillium *Trillium ovatum* I rebirth my feminine
Wahclella Falls I birth myself anew in the presence of the nature spirits
Western Redcedar *Thuja plicata* I am a Tree of Life
Western Rhododendron *Rhododendron macrophyllum* I enhance my experience of compassion
White Salmon River I remember! I am wild and free
Wild Rose *Rosa pisocarpa* I am passionate about life
Willow *Salix spp.* I flow with forgiveness
Yarrow *Achillea millefolium* I am pure & strong

For more information on these wildflowers and where to find them, I recommend Russ Jolley's book, *A Comprehensive Field Guide: Wildflowers of the Columbia Gorge*, Oregon Historical Society Press.

Glossary

Ancestors are the spirit of ancient ones with earth memories that live in the trees, lands, and waters, and earth, the indigenous spirits who have lived on earth previously, and our personal ancestors.

Ascension gradual or sudden process of bringing and holding higher frequencies of light in the physical body to reach a place of enlightenment and ability to dwell in higher dimensions of love—4th and 5th dimension.

Astral Projection the ability to perceive the traveling of our astral body outside our own physical body.

Auric Fields consist of energetic fields, or layers, that surround and infuse the body like an invisible egg. Each layer of our aura corresponds to a different aspect of our being: etheric body (physical), emotional body, mental body, astral body, etheric body, celestial body, and ketheric/causal bodies. The layers relate with our chakra system. The health of our aura reflects our health and sense of self including boundaries, immunity, and protection.

Central Channel the subtle life-force, divine, and earth energy that flows in the center of the body connecting above, below, and all chakras together. The central channel, also called rainbow bridge or Sushumna, is a bridge between our highest spiritual connection and physical embodiment.

Chakra is a Sanskrit word for *wheel*. Chakras are the seats of spiritual and emotional power in our body. Like wheels of subtle energetic light, they circulate with subtle light energy. Seven major chakras include: 1st root—foundation, grounding, 2nd sacral—emotional center, 3rd solar plexus—personal power center, 4th heart—love, compassion, 5th throat—communication, 6th 3rd eye—intuition, visions, 7th crown—universal connection. There are also numerous chakras in the body including ones in the hands, feet, above and below body.

Channeling communicating with the spirit of nature, angelic or fairy realms, ancestors, and spiritual beings to bring through transmissions of energy, information, wisdom, guidance, healing, and inspiration.

Clairaudience ability to intuit based on hearing and perceiving sound, tones, songs, vibrations and words beyond normal hearing.

Clairsentience ability to intuit and know through feelings, sensations, emotions, feelings, touch, and qualities of energy movement.

Clairvoyance ability to see images, auras, colors, invisible realms, and perceive based on visual stimuli through the 3rd eye.

Deva a large being of nature that patterns, oversees, and organizes fairies, nature spirits, and elementals in the landscape. There are Devas of mountains, forests, valleys, and areas of land and water. The Devic realms are in-between angelic and nature realms. Devas is also a term used broadly to describe many angelic and nature beings that help humanity, and it is used inter-changeably for describing the spirit of a plant—the Deva of a plant.

Doctrine of Signatures the healing pattern, or *signature*, a plant reveals by its shape, color, habitat, growth pattern, and gesture. For example, a plant with heart-shaped flowers reveals its connection to healing of the heart.

Dosage Bottle a bottle containing a flower essence or formula that was created by adding any amount of drops from one or more stock essence(s) in water and a preservative.

Dowsing a technique used to ask questions and receive answers intuitively through divination. A pendulum and finger kinesiology are two methods described in this book that use dowsing to answer "yes" or "no" questions. Water divination and witching are dowsing divination techniques.

Elements all of creation is made of elements of Earth, Fire, Water, Air, and Ethers.

Elementals forms of nature spirits that are creative beings associated with Earth, Fire, Water, Air. Traditionally, the associations were Earth—gnomes, Fire—salamanders, Water—undines, and Air—sylphs.

Emotional Empathy intuitive understanding and knowing through emotional connection and merging with feeling, sensing, and emotions.

Fairy a spirit associated with nature and used to describe spirit beings associated with flowers, plants, trees, land, water, crystals, etc. Fairy is used interchangeably with nature spirit.

Geopathic Stress *geo* means *earth*. Geopathic stress comes from EMF (electro-magnetic frequencies) and other means that gather in ley lines of earth causing distorted energy fields. It can disturb land, homes, places, and people.

Intention focusing a thought, attention, and energy mindfully on something.

Medicine used in an indigenous or plant person's context to signify anything of nature that is healing. *Medicine person* is someone who is a healer and uses shamanism and indigenous ways to bring healing through. Carrying certain kinds of *medicine* means you are gifted in that way.

Mental Empathy ability to communicate by transferring thoughts back and forth without speaking. A sense of intuitive knowing and interpreting thoughts and what is in the mind.

Mother Essence the original water that was used to create a flower essence with preservative added.

Nature Spirits beings that dwell in the invisible realms of nature that animate plants, animals, waters. Some people used term interchangeably with fairies and Devas.

Purification clearing and cleansing of the subtle energy field of emotional, mental, and spiritual energies.

Qi (Chi) life-force energy.

Rites of Passage celebrating life passages (first moon-time, manhood, motherhood, croning, etc.) with intentional activities, celebrations, ceremony, ritual, or practices.

Sacred Geometry the sacred invisible design of the universe that creates energy and form through patterns such as the flower of life.

Shaman someone who walks between spiritual and physical worlds.

Shadow Aspect a denied or hidden aspect of the self.

Starseed one who comes from the stars, another planet, or place in the cosmos with the purpose of assisting the earth's and humanity's ascension.

Stock Essence a bottle of flower essence made by placing seven drops from the *Mother Essence* into water and preservative.

Subtle Energy invisible earth and spiritual life-force energy that flows through everyone and everything.

Succuss gentle tapping of a bottle on the palm of the hand to shake its contents and activate its strength.

Teleportation transportation of our body without relying on physical means.

Tree of Life symbolizes interconnectivity of all of Creation through time and space—roots and branches. Mirrors inner-life and body in spiritual traditions. Connects heaven (spiritual world) and earth (material world).

Vibrational Medicine using subtle energy frequencies to heal and align another's energy frequencies. Vibrational medicine includes flower essences, gem essences or elixirs, crystals, sound, homeopathy.

Vision Quest taking time out of mundane life to ceremonially cross into a spiritual landscape to seek a vision or purpose for life.

Yin, Yang used in Chinese Medicine to describe feminine Qi earth energy, masculine Qi life-force energy.

Flower Essences and Elements

EARTH
Angelica, Balsamroot, California Poppy, Desert Sage, Fairy Slipper Orchid, Foxglove, Green Bog Orchid, Heart-leaf Buckwheat, Moss, Mullein, Oregon Oak, Poet's Shooting Star, Ponderosa Pine, Queen Bead Lily, Red-flowering Currant, Western Redcedar, Wild Rose

FIRE
Balsamroot, Barrett's Penstemon, Buttercup, California Poppy, Desert Sage, Foxglove, Mullein, Oregon Grape, Ponderosa Pine, Pungent Desert Parsley, Red Columbine, Tiger Lily

WATER
Ball-head Waterleaf, California Poppy, Camas, Desert Sage, Fairy Slipper Orchid, Mock Orange, Moss, Mt Hood Lily, Mullein, Ocean Spray, Phantom Orchid, Queen Bead Lily, Red-flowering Currant, Tiger Lily, Trillium, Western Redcedar, Willow

AIR
Angelica, Ball-head Waterleaf, Barrett's Penstemon, Bleeding Heart, California Poppy, Desert Sage, Larkspur, Mock Orange, Mullein, Phantom Orchid, Poet's Shooting Star, Ponderosa Pine, Pungent Desert Parsley, Queen Bead Lily, Silky Lupine, Western Rhododendron

ETHERS
California Poppy, Desert Sage, Mullein

Flower Essences for Chakras

1st Chakra - Root
Barrett's Penstemon, Buttercup, Green Bog Orchid, Oregon Grape, Oregon Oak, Poet's Shooting Star, Red-flowering Currant, Tiger Lily, Western Redcedar, Wild Rose, Willow

2nd Chakra - Sacral
Fairy Slipper Orchid, Mock Orange, Mt Hood Lily, Ocean Spray, Oregon Oak, Phantom Orchid, Ponderosa Pine, Queen Bead Lily, Red-flowering Currant, Tiger Lily, Trillium, Western Redcedar

3rd Chakra - Solar Plexus
Ball-head Waterleaf, Balsamroot, Buttercup, California Poppy, Heart-leaf Buckwheat, Mullein, Oregon Grape, Oregon Oak, Pungent Desert Parsley, Red Columbine, Western Redcedar, W. Rhododendron, Willow

4th Chakra - Heart
Bleeding Heart, California Poppy, Desert Sage, Fairy Slipper Orchid, Foxglove, Green Bog Orchid, Heart-leaf Buckwheat, Larkspur, Moss, Mt Hood Lily, Mullein, Oregon Grape, Oregon Oak, Phantom Orchid, Ponderosa Pine, Pungent Desert Parsley, Queen Bead Lily, Red-flowering Currant, Trillium, Western Redcedar, Western Rhododendron, Wild Rose, Willow, Yarrow

5th Chakra - Throat
California Poppy, Desert Sage, Green Bog Orchid, Larkspur, Oregon Oak, Silky Lupine, Tiger Lily, Western Redcedar, Yarrow

6th Chakra - 3rd Eye
Balsamroot, Buttercup, California Poppy, Camas, Desert Sage, Fairy Slipper Orchid, Green Bog Orchid, Mullein, Oregon Oak, Trillium, Western Redcedar, Wild Rose

7th Chakra - Crown
Angelica, Ball-head Waterleaf, Fairy Slipper Orchid, Heart-leaf Buckwheat, Moss, Oregon Oak, Phantom Orchid, Queen Bead Lily, Western Redcedar, Wild Rose, Yarrow

More Flower Essences

Apple Tree *Malus pumila* promotes happiness, mental clarity, joyful optimism, goddess consciousness and return of *Avalon,* unicorn tree.

Ball-head Cluster Lily *Brodiaea congesta* awakens clairvoyance, intuitive development, clears mind and 3rd eye, opens heart, awakens creative inspiration, addresses self-sabotage, adjusts perspective, lily-feminine principle.

Bristlecone Pine Tree *Pinus longaeva* (California) brings ancient wisdom, ancestral roots and grounding, right relationship with earth, timelessness, communication with plant realms, conduit of source energy, 8,000 year-old mother earthkeeper tree.

Calendula *Calendula officinalis* opens communication with nature spirits, softens communication, confidence, radiance of 3rd chakra, solar energy, dragon and fire flower.

Chocolate Lily *Fritillaria affinis* assists in deepening our grounding practice and relationship to the earth, helps one address issues of how to feel *safe* in the body—embodiment, awakens abundance consciousness, lily-feminine principle.

Corn, Hopi *Zea Mays* strengthens spiritual relationship with the earth, builds energy life-force, nurtures new patterns of receptivity, opens ability to receive nourishment.

Cosmos *Cosmos bipinnatus* enables clearer expression and communication, provides a celestial bridge to connect and communicate with cosmic energies.

Dandelion *Taraxacum officinale* fosters resilience and a sunny disposition, moves anger and liver congestion and supports all liver functions and digestive fire, relaxes and loosens the physical body.

Dogbane, Hemp *Apocynum cannabinum* provides shamanic revelation of unconscious motivations, awareness of personal energy leaks, creates time and space for life re-evaluation.

Elderberry *Sambucus cerulea* facilitates ancestor healing, honor and access memories, remembering origins, support becoming an elder, immunity.

Flax, Blue *Linum perenne* activates ability to change the mind and believe and see new things, assists in moving beyond limitations of thought, belief, or conditioning.

Glacier Lily *Erythronium grandiflorum* supports healthy joyful self-expression, addresses soul hiding, lends a sense of protection, trust in power of love for sensitive souls, lily-feminine principle.

Grass Widow *Sisyrinchium douglasii* promotes self-reliance, freedom from co-dependence, heals sense of separation from Source including divorce or abandonment, dance into new self-image, inner-child, trust issues, new beginnings.

Hawthorne Tree *Crataegus douglasii var. douglassi* signifies healing for contracted heart energy, enlivens spine to receive earth and life-force energy, enhances belief in (and sense of) spiritual love and our divinity, offers stress release, eases excess striving, addresses trust issues, teaches how to let go, sacred to the Celtic people, Celtic portal-shamanic journey tree.

Indian Pipe *Monotropa uniflora* represents the *peace pipe*, awakens self-love and peace between all people and all nations, unity in diversity, expansion of capacity to receive love, also called Ghost Pipe.

Lavender *Lavadula officianalis* awakens spirituality, balances extremes, calms mind and heart.

Maple Tree, Bigleaf *Acer macrophyllum* supports new growth, yin/yang balance, restores harmony.

Marigold *Tagetes* connects spirits to our altars, flower of life and death, life-death cycle, ancestors, communication across the veils, abundant life blessings, honored in traditions Samhain (Celtic New Year), Mexican Dia de Muertos.

Paintbrush, Harsh *Castilleja hispida* helps to ground and express creative potential in daily life, creativity.

Pink Yarrow *Achillea millefolium var. rosea* offers protection for energetically sensitive and overly compassionate souls that tend to absorb energies, thoughts, and emotions of others. Brings greater awareness to energy of relationships as it strengthens auric boundaries and co-dependent tendencies. Great for empaths. Soothing for the heart. Confidence building.

Prairie Star *Lithophragma parviflora* bestows self-love, gently opens rock-hard energy blocks, fairies work collectively to help awaken more love.

Queen Anne's Lace *Daucus carota* grounds intuition and the 3rd eye during spiritual openings, offers clarity, clairvoyance, balances and stabilizes expanded states of awareness, helps us see what is hidden.

Rosemary *Rosmarinus officinalis* (Sedona) assists with embodiment, supports relationship closure and honoring of the past, assists energy integration in the body, trauma clearing to bring spirit back to the body.

St John's Wort *Hypericum perforatum* light giver, fire and solar power, enlightens cells from fear, lifts depression, calm nightmares, etheric protection in dreamtime.

Teasel *Dipsacus sylvesfris* builds an energy fortress, supports self-sovereignty, energetic integrity, seal leaks in energy system (chakras), may assist with Lyme disease.

Violet *Viola odorata* comforts, moves and heals grief, emotionally uplifting, heart-opening sweetness and healing, honors our sensitivity, supports shy and subtle aspects of the self.

Wild Ginger *Asarum caudatum* activates the root chakra, offers grounding and resistance to grounding, helps us feel safe in body, healing of sexual abuse.

White Rose *Rosa species* brings spiritual awakening, devotion, compassion, spiritual purity, faith, unconditional love of the mother.

Acknowledgements & Gratitude

I want to acknowledge and thank all those who shared teachings and wisdom with me and helped bring this book and my flower essences into being. Thank you to the wildflowers, tree, waters, and sacred places of the Columbia River Gorge and The Ancestors of these beautiful lands. Thank you to the First Peoples of these lands the Yakama, Nez Perce, Celilo Wyam, Klickitat, Confederated Tribes of Warm Springs, and other tribes. This book, and this body of work, would not exist without you. Thank you to all my teachers, elders, colleagues, apprentices, students, clients, and customers over many years. There are too many to name. Thank you to the International Council of Thirteen Indigenous Grandmothers especially three important teachers in my life: Grandmother Marie Alice Campos Freire, Grandmother Flordemayo, and Grandmother Agnes Baker Pilgrim. Thank you to Marshall "Golden Eagle" Jack, Marilyn and Tohmas Twintreess, and Grandmother Judith Moore. Thanks to Flower Essence Services, Dr. Bach, Gurudas, and all the flower essence makers, practitioners, writers, and sources that share information. Thank you to the Fairy & Human Relations Congress organizers and teachers. Thank you to Daysha Eaton, Sandy Hawke, Joy Olson, Stacey Croton, Carlin Wigham, Kim Lindemyer, Ani Sinclair, Kathrin Huber, Shannon Tortolano, Lance Koudele, Riki Chodowski, Nancy Napp, Cindy Jack, Katie Silva, Heather Kowalewski, Abby Kenny, Elyssa Jakim, Saliha Abrams, Sherry Dell, Richard Bryant, Robbee Lapp, Ellen Trichter, Erin Grover, Andrea Dombecki, Karen Folgarelli, Dani Palacio, Kim Steffgen, Christopher Vaeth, Erico Schleicher, Scott and Kathryn Dusseau Kloos, Nicole Pepper, Wells Bishop, and the many others who helped me, and this work, grow. Thank you to those who contributed their stories to these pages to help illuminate the ways plant spirits and the flower essences can help us grow. Finally, thank you to my family and friends for their on-going love and support including those that reside in the *green realms*.

Camilla Blossom Bishop

Camilla delights in singing, dancing, co-creating, and communing with the spirits of nature. She cultivates relationships with nature elementals, plants, lands, and waters where she lives and in her travels. Her passion is to inspire others to come into loving relationship with the spirit of nature and connect with the abundance of Mother Earth. She helps catalyze people's lineage gifts and ability to co-create relationship and healing with nature spirits, nature elementals (nature spirits of Earth, Fire, Water, Earth, Ethers), fairies, mermaids, unicorns, gnomes, dragons, flower fairies, water Devas, tree guardians, and ancient ancestors. She holds deep gratitude for the *green realms*. Camilla is a Nature Spirit Alchemist, Flower Essence Alchemist, Intuitive Energy Healer, teacher, and writer. She lives at Prairie Star Meadows in Mosier, Oregon and loves to spend time in The Unicorn Garden.

Nature Spirit Alchemy - Products & Services

Sacred Spirit of The Gorge: Columbia River Gorge Flower Essences and Essences (book)
Sacred Spirit Deck Explore the plants & places of The Columbia River Gorge (44-card photographic deck, booklet, box)
Kit: 44 Columbia River Gorge Flower Essences (available individually)
Flower Essences, Flower Essence Formulas, & Sprays
Nature Mentoring
Healing Services
Blog
Events
Unicorn Garden Club

NatureSpiritAlchemy.com
CamillaBlossom.com
ETSY shop: www.Etsy.com/shop/NatureSpiritAlchemy

Made in the USA
San Bernardino, CA
12 July 2017